lime
green

Cover photo by Sharon & Nikki McCutcheon.
Book design by Anton Khodakovsky.

HIS Publishing Group
1402 Corinth St., Suite 131
Dallas, TX 75215

HIS Publishing Group is a division of Human Improvement Specialists, llc. For information visit www.hispubg.com or contact publisher at info@hispubg.com

Library of Congress Control Number:
2015909182

ISBN-13:
978-0-578-16505-9

lime green

Reshaping Our View of Women in the Church

DR. JACKIE ROESE

www.hispubg.com

A division of HISpecialists, llc

ENDORSEMENTS

Dr. Jackie Roese's candidness and humor in sharing her journey and experiences in ministry are refreshing and greatly needed in evangelical circles today. This is not a book with any agenda other than Jackie's own words, "I am a follower of Jesus Christ doing my very best to be obedient to Him...that's who I am." In our journey to know and serve Jesus, gender should be embraced and edify the Body of Christ. Dr. Roese eloquently and theologically communicates this and demonstrates practical ways for women in ministry to do the same. My hope is that this book will help others in their journeys as well. Men and women alike can learn much from this refreshing read!

—**Deborah Fikes**, Representative to the United Nations for the
World Evangelical Alliance (WEA)

Every follower of Christ is given gifts by the Holy Spirit for the building up of the church. And the same gifts are given to both men and women. Jackie Roese is a gifted leader and teacher who has an important story to tell about finding her gifts and using them for the building up of the body of Christ. In this book Jackie tells her story with characteristic courage and candor. It's an important story that will challenge and inspire anyone who reads it.

—**Barry D. Jones**, Associate Professor of Pastoral Ministries, Dallas
Theological Seminary and Associate Teaching Pastor, Irving Bible Church

The beauty of this story is it's not just about God's redemptive work in the life of one woman. It's about how God has used the voice of a woman to so impact men and women that it begs the question: what in the world does God intend to do through women? Jackie's journey to the pulpit is a journey full of questions and struggle, faith-family courage, risk, and pain. But it is also a journey that has brought about unexpected and immeasurable life. It is most certainly worth the read.

—**Betsy Nichols**, Employee Engagement Architect, Symbolist and Preaching Team Member, Irving Bible Church

Jackie Roese's story is poignant, her reasoning is sharp, and her vision is compelling. As one committed to biblical exegesis and kingdom theology, I am inspired by Jackie's call to new creation thinking and partnerships. Count on it: this book is going to stir up a new generation of young women and men. To God be the glory.

—**Ray Befus**, Pastor and Regional Leader, Great Lakes North, Vineyard USA

DEDICATION

To my husband Steve

You are my ennobler. You have done whatever necessary for me to live out God's call on my life. When I wanted to shrink back you encouraged me forward. When I was tired you carried the load.

You sacrificed.

You have not only cherished but also challenged me to live large for Jesus. And you have done the same for so many other women in the conservative faith community. You truly live out the "Blessed Alliance."

We need more men like you.

TABLE OF CONTENTS

FOREWORD

THOSE IN POWER perpetuate themselves. This is the way things have been, the way things are and the way things will be, unless those in power put down their power to empower those not in power. Let me translate: Males are in power and perpetuate male power, and unless they put down their male power and empower women, male power will continue to dominate. This is true even in the church, where there shouldn't be a question of power, but there all too often is.

There is God the Father, God the Son, and God the Holy Spirit. Early theologians called the relationship of the Father, Son and Spirit *perichoresis*, which as a term describes not hierarchy and not power but mutual indwelling in the endless dance of self-sacrificing love for the others. That's *Who God Is*, not what God does. If God is like that, the church that has been created by this Father-Son-Spirit ought also to be perichoretic. In other words, our God was not a power-perpetuating God but a power-surrendering God.

Now the problem. As Jackie Roese describes in this story full of pathos and love and twists and turns and reality, males created a narrative that women are to be Pink. Which is fine for women who are Pink. But Jackie is not alone in being Lime Green. (I must say now that I have described such women as blue parakeets, but that's another story that tells the same story.) Lime Green women don't do Pink well. And Pink males in power don't know what to make of Lime Green women.

I know because I was once a Pink-preferring male and then I became a silent Lime Green supporter. Silent support is betrayal. Lime Green women need Lime Green males to have sufficient courage to stand up for the gifts God's Spirit is giving to women today.

Lime Green Jackie discovered that God had gifted her to think critically, to ponder theology for herself, and to study and preach the Bible as God had called her. Lime Green now clashes with male power in churches that perpetuate male power and not cruciform gospel living. Jackie and the leaders at Irving Bible Church took time to ponder a colossal set of questions in a colossal cultural context that was created by male power self-perpetuating. They did well and concluded not only that God had gifted Jackie – and anyone who reads this book knows she's got the gifts to teach and preach – but that the Bible challenged their perpetuating system. So they took a step out in faith, freedom and courage to put Jackie behind the pulpit.

She tells that story in this book, but perhaps the hidden highlights are that she moves seamlessly from her very tough childhood into a faith for which she had no preparation, with a man who is himself gifted and patient and loving, and three children who present their own challenges… and physical pains and church pains and theological pains… and she gives us a wonderful story of what it is really like for the woman who discovers she's gifted to preach and teach in a church that isn't so sure.

All women gifted to teach will be encouraged by Jackie's story; all churches wondering about women with such gifts will be challenged by this book; and all moms who have daughters will find this book thrilling and exciting of what God is doing in our time.

I'm doubly proud I know Steve and Jackie, and I hope you will be moved as much as I was in reading this book. What a gift to the church today.

Scot McKnight
Julius R. Mantey Professor in New Testament
Northern Seminary

INTRODUCTION

Lime Green is *not* a book making the case for women preachers (or any other leadership role for that matter). Rather, it's a story about me, a clueless farm girl who stumbled into vocational Christian work. I ended up bumping into walls, crossing invisible lines, and ultimately reshaping my view of women—and my church's view, too. I hope my story of stumbling and bumping can make other women's journeys a bit smoother.

Lime Green is for women who find themselves serving Jesus (or longing to serve him) in conservative faith communities. I'm not talking about women who are paid with a title or women who are on staff at a specific Christian organization or church—that's too limiting. Too many women serve in ministries without a title, position, pay, or recognition. *Lime Green* is for women who serve Jesus in *any* capacity in conservative faith communities.

As women who serve in these ministries, we face unique challenges at home and work. Many times those challenges are directly related to our gender. We have too few role models, too few places to ask questions, raise concerns, or express doubts. We have limited church resources and few opportunities to develop our skills. Many of us have lived isolated ministry lives, silently frustrated by the lack of opportunities for our gender, feeling misunderstood and undervalued by our church leaders. We desperately want to serve Jesus with every fiber of our being but aren't sure how to go about it. This is a book about changing that, revealing a way, a path with all its rocks, hills, and smooth road, to help others find their footing in reshaping the way we view women. That change must happen in you first!

Lime Green will challenge—or perhaps allow you to breathe a sigh of relief over—your view of yourself. It will break down the idea that we must all conform to that all too elusive concept of the "ideal biblical woman." Too many of us already know that we aren't that woman, but we pretend. We put on our light pink sheepskin and play pretend. Our churches are filled with light pink ladies, or at least women in light pink sheepskins.

Let me explain what I mean.

Coming to Dallas as a brand-new Christian who had never been around other Christians nor really attended any church, I quickly learned Christian women are supposed to be light pink. That's the color I saw when I went to my first women's Bible study in North Dallas at Northwest Bible Church. I'm known for saying, "Texas women know how to be women!" That's what I saw. Women, dressed to the nines with shoes, bags, and jewelry to match. Their makeup tastefully done. Their fingernails well manicured. Many of the older women had nicer figures than my young twenty-something shape. (I later learned you can *buy* that better shape.)

The women seemed quieter, nicer—True Blue Southern Belles. I, on the other hand, just got off the boat, so to speak, from New York. Sarcasm, directness, and swearing were normative for northeasterners. When we speak, we go from Point A to Point B. But light pink women (these southern Christian women) take you upstream, around the barn, through the woods before stating what they want. And even when they said something unpleasant, you didn't realize it because it was wrapped with a smile and a "bless your soul." I found it exhausting.

My hair was unruly. I never really learned how to manage my wild mane. (Later, I would learn it's all about products.) I didn't wear makeup. I had never had a manicure, nor did I own a fancy purse. I found backpacks to be way more functional. I felt like I was in a foreign country.

Over time, I came to see these women as more than just nails and purses. They were kind, caring women. They had dignity and they served each other and the church very well. They could "get things done." You just didn't know they were doing it. What was most evident was that these women really loved Jesus. Over time I found myself thinking, *If I'm going to be a good Christian woman, then I need to be more like them. I need to get some makeup, a red purse, and I need to be nicer and quieter!*

I thought I needed to be light pink.

Later, as I served in the church, it became evident that we promote light pink ladies as the ideal biblical woman. Light pink women are married with kids. Their work is to undergird their husband and children. They stay at home and create a warm, hospitable space for others. They serve at their church in the nursery, children's church, women's ministry, or on a hospitality team. And they look good doing it. And lest you think I'm only talking about churches in Texas: though my experience was in the South, I eventually found this ideal of the biblical woman alive and well all across America.

Listen to one prominent theologian list the qualities of the ideal biblical woman. She's "responsive, compassionate, empathetic, enduring, gentle, warm, tender, hospitable, receptive, diplomatic, considerate, polite, supportive, intuitive, wise, perceptive, sensitive, spiritual, sincere, vulnerable (in the sense of emotionally open), obedient, trusting, graceful, sweet, expressive, charming, delicate, quiet, sensually receptive (vs. prudish), faithful, pure."[1]

Do you hear the way we view women? Light pink. Of course, I'm not against light pink ladies. It certainly is one way women express who God is, but it's not the only way. Thank goodness. Or, I'd be disqualified from being a Christian woman and failing at expressing an image of God.

Charming, sweet, delicate, quiet, sensually receptive? I'm out. What's even more disheartening is that I identify more with this particular theologian's description of male attributes: "Theology and church and mission are marked by overarching godly male leadership in the spirit of Christ, with an ethos of tender-hearted strength, and contrite courage, and risk-taking decisiveness, and readiness to sacrifice for the sake of leading, protecting, and providing for the community."[2]

---

1   John Piper and Wayne Grudem, eds., *Rediscovering Biblical Manhood and Womanhood* (Wheaton, Ill: Crossway, 2006) p. 46.

2   John Piper, "'The Frank and Manly Mr. Ryle' — The Value of a Masculine Ministry," *Desiring God,* January 31, 2012, desiringgod.org/biographies/the-frank-and-manly-mr-ryle-the-value-of-a-masculine-ministry

What's a lime green woman to do in her faith community? Especially when we prefer light pink ladies because they make us feel safer, not just among our male leadership but also other women in our congregations. Unfortunately, women can sometimes be other women's greatest adversaries.

An older woman sat across from me. She wanted to "share some concerns" she had about my teaching. She told me that she represented the older women—"the 1950s women"—in our church. As her comments progressed, she questioned my dress, my hairstyle, and my tendency to roam the stage while I talked. "That's the way men teach," she said. In no uncertain terms, she let me know that I was viewed as "aggressive." She told me that my level of training—and my confidence—was creating tension for other women. She and her friends stayed home and made sure there was breakfast and dinner on the table. She assumed my level of training and job responsibilities precluded me from caring for my family in the same fashion. I didn't tell her I too cooked breakfast for my kids, packed their school lunches, and cooked dinners from scratch. We have ideas and ideals about what a Christian woman is supposed to be like, and when a woman doesn't fit into those ideals, we feel unsafe.

—

Recently my daughter Madison called from college, *"Mom, you didn't teach me anything growing up! You didn't teach me how to make a wreath or plant a garden."*

"Well, I taught you how to think," I told her.

"I could have learned that in college!"

I suggested if she wanted to learn those things she should get in her car and drive herself to her grandma's. She did just that. Madison's college is about an hour-and-a-half from my mom's home in Upstate N.Y. That's one of the reasons she chose to go to Bennington College in Vermont, to be close to my mom. They spent their weekend in the woods looking for vines to make wreaths and planting and harvesting in my mom's garden. My mom could rival Martha Stewart. On Sunday I received a picture of their newly-made wreaths and a hot-out-of-the-oven strawberry rhubarb pie. (My mom is the best pie maker on earth!)

My mom raised us five kids while caring for several other kids, too. She worked alongside my dad in our family business and kept a very clean home. Not an easy task for a farm family. She used a large box of laundry detergent every week. Six loads of laundry every day! She cooked home-cooked meals three times a day, and she did summer canning so we could eat well in the winter. I never once heard my mom complain, gossip, or raise her voice in anger.

My mom—the most influential woman in my life—is light pink. Mom is a woman of beauty. She's physically beautiful, but more importantly, she creates beauty wherever she is. She places herself among beauty and sees it in everything and everyone.

Beauty. Peace. Safety.

That's what you experience when you are around her.

I'm nothing like my mother.

I'm lime green.[3] I can't decorate, don't like to shop, and think serving home-made spaghetti out of the pot is setting a nice table. But, lime green women get in the foxhole. They carry you on their shoulders to safety. They aren't afraid of the hard or the mess in life. Lime green women are not necessarily sweet or peaceful and many times not all that "polite." In fact they tend to be more like the Old Testament prophets, saying the hard things when no one wants to hear it.

In his book, *The Barbarian Way*, Irwin McManus describes what I see as lime green when he writes about Jephthah the Gileadite from Judges 11:1–11. It's a story of three brothers, two of whom viewed Jephthah as a threat. Because of this, they ousted him from the city. Jephthah went to live among the barbarians and became an excellent warrior. Later, when the city came under siege, they begged Jephthah to come back and fight for the city.

---

3   I'm not sure why this color came to me. But I see lime green as warm, yet bold. Wooing, yet a bit dangerous. It's passionate.

McManus writes, "Barbarians are not welcome among the civilized and are feared among the domesticated (he argues our churches have become too domesticated – or, if you will, civilized)... Barbarians can be counted as worthless when all is safe and secure, but dangerous times suddenly make them invaluable."[4]

Barbarians are lime green.

Warriors. Truth Tellers. Passionate. (How many times have women said, "I'm more like a man than a woman?" Ugh.)[5]

Dr. Sarah Sumner, Dean of the A.W. Tozer Theological Seminary at Simpson University, states when a woman has "male qualities," she is encouraged to hold back those qualities when around men. If she doesn't, she is viewed several ways: trying to prove herself as good as a man, an insecure, needy woman or worse yet, a feminist.[6]

Lime Green invites us to take off our light pink sheepskin.

When we try to tint ourselves a shade or color that doesn't suit us, we deny God's creativity. He said we are each fearfully and wonderfully made, a one-of-a-kind, never-to-be-seen-again-in-history person (Psalm 139). We deny his creativity and we ignore his Word.

God saved you by his grace when you believed. And you can't take credit for this; it is a gift from God. Salvation is not a reward for the good things we have done, so none of us can boast about it. Ephesians 2:8–10 says, "*For we are God's masterpiece. He has created us anew in Christ Jesus, so we can do the good things he planned for us long ago*" (Italics mine).

---

4   Irwin McManus, *The Barbarian Way* (Nashville: Thomas Nelson, 2005) pp. 15–16.

5   Following are some suggestions from a college sociology textbook. (By Pearson Education, Inc.)
Feminine Traits: Submissive, Dependent, Unintelligent and Incapable Emotional, Receptive, Intuitive, Weak, Timid, Content, Passive, Cooperative, Sensitive, Sex object, Attractive because of physical appearance. Masculine Traits: Dominant, Independent, Intelligent and Competent, Rational, Assertive, Analytical, Strong, Brave, Ambitious, Active, Competitive, Insensitive, Sexually aggressive, Attractive because of achievement.

6   Sarah Sumner, *Men and Women in the Church* (Downers Grove, Ill: InterVarsity Press, 2003), pp. 27, 73–73, 79.

One young seminary graduate shared how her faith community's view of women shaped their view of her work.

You are never really able to notice that something is the way it is until you begin to compare it against something or someone else. That is what happened with me. I didn't really realize the way I was being treated when I initially came on board the staff at my church, until another male counterpart was hired. I noticed that treatment was different mainly from the other pastors. When they saw him, they would give him a handshake, but when they saw me there was no handshake and just a nice nod and smile. At first, it didn't really get to me, but when it happens more than occasionally you can't help but notice and start having a very bad feeling in your gut. You want to ignore it and you give yourself a positive self-talk, but at a certain point you realize that it really does bother you. Then there is the question. It seems that most every time I am asked a question it has something more to do with whether I would like to be married and what my future plans are in the domestic arena. However, it is completely a different story for my male counterpart. He is asked what his future plans in ministry are. Now, it is not that I have anything against being domestic or getting married. In fact, I love being domestic and definitely want to get married in the near future! My frustration comes in the fact that I am also not asked what my future plans in ministry will be. Why is it hard to see that God might want to use my life in just the same way that he would in any male pastor's life? One of my dreams in ministry is for all the pastors to see me as full of potential for a future in ministry and letting the first question they ask me be "What are your future plans in ministry?" instead of "Are you planning to get married soon?"

A one-of-a-kind, never-to-be-seen-again person whose design is perfectly suited to do "good works" planned for them by God. What if those good works aren't changing babies in the nursery? Or cooking a meal in the church kitchen? What if they are different than the ideal promoted in our faith communities?

Again, McManus' words are helpful: "When you understand what Jesus means when He says you must follow Him, you finally realize this is not a cattle call. He is not calling you to the same life everyone else will live. He's not even calling you to the same path every follower of Christ will walk. Your life is unique before God, and your path is yours and yours alone. Where God will choose to lead you and how God chooses to use your life cannot be predicted by how God has worked in the lives of others before you."[7]

Reshaping our view means embracing how God made us and doing the work he gave us—for his glory.

In the Bible, God said we are to bring him glory. That's our purpose: to glorify God (see Isaiah 43:7 and Romans 11:36). Take note: the Bible doesn't say our purpose is to mother or be married or work or serve in a specific space or place. Too often we hear those spoken and unspoken messages about our role as women. Our roles as wife, mother, supporter. The problem is most women in our pews don't identify with that stereotype.

Today 51 percent of women in America live without a spouse, and 71 percent of women with children under the age of 18 work outside the home. Forty years ago women owned five percent of small business. Now they own thirty. Forty percent of women say they have more opportunity to lead outside their churches than within them.

In 2011 a Barna study noted a steady decrease in women's church attendance over the past twenty years. Perhaps women leave church because they can't find their real life represented there. We need to stop limiting women by *our* limited definitions of womanhood as light pink only.

It's time to revisit the Bible and listen to God speak of how women embody the Imago Dei. Perhaps we feel fresh wind on our face as we hear whispers of a more perfect view.

---

7   Irwin McManus, *The Barbarian Way* (Nashville: Thomas Nelson, 2005), pp. 36–37.

God said he created us—male and female—to bring him glory. No his or her lists. How we glorify God is limitless, open-ended. I'll explain why in a minute. But first, consider what glory means:

To give weight or the exhibition of God's excellence.

To exhibit God's beauty, character and infinite worth.

Consider all of who God is.

How can one color (or one gender with a list of characteristics attributed to that gender) possibly express all of who God is? Not possible, right?

O LORD, our Lord, how majestic is your name in all the earth!

You have set your glory above the heavens.

From the lips of children and infants you have ordained praise because of your enemies, to silence the foe and the avenger.

When I consider your heavens, the work of your fingers, the moon and the stars, which you have set in place, what is man that you are mindful of him, the son of man that you care for him?

You made him a little lower than the heavenly beings and crowned him with glory and honor.

You made him ruler over the works of your hands; you put everything under his feet: all flocks and herds, and the beasts of the field, the birds of the air, and the fish of the sea, all that swim the paths of the seas.

O LORD, our Lord, how majestic is your name in all the earth!

—Psalm 8

It would take every color we've ever seen—and even colors we haven't seen—and every shade of those colors to exhibit all of who God is. Each of us, in our own shade of color, says something about who God is to the world in ways others don't or can't in quite the same fashion. Peace. Beauty. Warrior. Truth teller. Notice God didn't give specific colors to specific genders. It's one big color wheel, and gender isn't in the equation.

What happens when a woman embraces her color?

How does our embracing our authentic color – unapologetically who we are – controlled by the Spirit, impact our Christian brothers' view of women? How can we help our brothers view us as partners and allies instead of a threat to their masculinity or a temptation to their morality? *Lime Green* is that story. It's my story, but in so many ways it's yours, too. You may not have picked corn in the fields nor preached from the pulpit, but you trip over gender wires, you've balanced the demands of family and ministry life, and you've bumped up against trials that just about took you out of the ministry. You have doubted, been lonely, and wondered if it was worth it. The plot and characters of your story may be different than mine, but the storyline is the same. We want to pour ourselves out for Jesus, so not a drop is left in our cup. But how? How do we women live fully alive, serving Jesus with everything we've got, within a conservative faith community?

"EMBRACE YOUR AUTHENTIC COLOR—UNAPOLOGETICALLY WHO YOU ARE—CONTROLLED BY THE SPIRIT."

We need light pink ladies who remind us that God is peace and beauty. But we also need you,

scarlet purple

bright red

soft yellow

sage green

cobalt blue.

Every color, every shade of color and colors we haven't even seen—yet—to remind us of everything else God is.

God is on the move. He's transforming our view of his Imago Dei—women. In the name of Jesus and for his kingdom sake. Amen.

Chapter One

NEVER A WASTE

IT WAS A HOT Texas morning in August of 2008. Sunday attendance was usually down in August, but not this day. On this day the sanctuary was filled to the brim, all two thousand two hundred and fifty seats. The air was filled with tension and anticipation. Channel 8's camera crew lined the back wall waiting to capture the "event" for the evening news. I sat in the front row, center left from the stage. Directly behind me was my husband, three kids, and a few close friends. My heart felt like it was beating outside my chest. It was a good thing I had an over-shirt on to hide the underarm sweat. Don't get me wrong: I was not afraid of preaching, I had preached hundreds of messages, but not to this crowd, not under these circumstances. Pastor Andy sat to my left and my bodyguard, Bryan, sat to my right. At a solid 5-foot-2, I tend to feel overpowered when standing next to men of Bryan's stature of 6-foot-5 and 230 pounds, but on this day I was comforted.

Dressed in black with a slicked back ponytail, arms crossed like a CIA agent, Bryan communicated to all present, *don't even think of trying to accost her.* There had been a lot of adversity building up to this day. The *Dallas Morning News* ran an article with my picture, "Woman's turn in the pulpit … brings buzz, beefs." A sister church alerted other conservative evangelical

1

pastors of the "grave moral concern" at Irving Bible Church (IBC). Mark Bailey, president of Dallas Theological Seminary, left our congregation, and his departure caused a stir at the seminary as well as churches pastored by former seminary students. The blogosphere went wild with affirmation and assailants alike. In light of this, our leadership decided Bryan should serve as my bodyguard for all three services. As the service began, my heart beat faster and faster. Jason, our worship pastor, took us to the throne through song. With all the chaos ensuing, I was never more grateful for song to center my mind and heart on Jesus. Just as Jason finished the last set, Pastor Andy walked up on stage and approached the podium. He welcomed everyone and then proceeded to share how the elders of IBC (all men), after a year and a half study, concluded women could preach from the pulpit. Then he asked the audience to welcome the first woman to preach in our church's 40-year history. Just before I got out of my seat, I turned to my fourteen-year-old daughter, "I want you to know I'm doing this for you and all the girls you represent, and I'm doing it for Jesus." Then with a deep breath I walked up on stage.

If someone had told my teenage self that someday I would stand in a pulpit and preach, I would have laughed in her face. Me? The girl with four siblings who grew up in Oneonta, New York, working on a farm without a clue about who God was? Never!

—

We didn't have a lot of money when I was in elementary school. Our yellow trailer sat smack in the middle of the open farm field my grandfather had given my dad. To the back right side of the trailer, Dad planted a garden of radishes, potatoes, cucumbers, and green beans. My grandfather slaughtered one of his pigs so we would have meat for the winter. Every December, my sister Daryl and I sold Christmas trees, standing in the often-blinding snow, hoping the customer wouldn't make us turn each tree—again and again—before deciding. Those Christmas trees bought groceries for the week.

When I was ten, my dad purchased farmland in Otego, New York, some fifteen minutes from our house. I loved that land, loved the drive down Route 7, the turn-off of the highway, and the little dirt road that led to the property.

At the bottom of our hill sat the small barn once used to slaughter pigs. A long rope with the huge metal hook used to drain blood from dead pigs still hung from the center of the ceiling. We kids would swing to one wall and push back with our feet, swinging back to the other side of the building.

Just beyond the slaughter barn, the ten-acre, wide-open field butted up against a bend in the Susquehanna River. Our first year of farming crops was hard work. My parents couldn't afford machinery or employees, which meant that we—Dad, Mom, Rod, Daryl, and I—were left to plant. My dad and Rod hoed, and my mom, sister, and I followed, bending over as we dropped the tiny seeds one by one. My dad offered a milkshake at the Big Dip ice-cream store as our reward for planting ten acres by hand.

Along with the ten acres of crops, Dad also built a small greenhouse off the back of our trailer. Each morning, I walked through the greenhouse to catch the bus. And every morning, I watched as the little seedlings turned into little plants, then larger ones. Dad kept growing flowers and the business. He bought the property on the hill above our trailer and rented some acreage down the road. It wasn't long before our ten acres grew to forty. But still, we had no machines or laborers besides us kids, who continued to bend over and plant one seed at a time.

Eventually our small farm grew to where we could sell our crops and plants at two different farm stands. We built our first fruit stand—a simple, brown, twenty-by-twenty structure—on the country road in front of our trailer. We rented the second from Ms. Gillingham, whose stand stood around the bend from the slaughterhouse on Route 7 in Otego.

My parents ran the store in Otego while Rod, Daryl, and I took care of the fruit stand in front of the trailer. My dad expected us to keep the peach table stacked and half-bushel baskets of apples full. He expected a clean place, floors swept, cooler wiped clean, and paper bags stacked nicely. He taught us the customer was always right.

Of course, we didn't always do what we were supposed to. Sometimes when my parents went away, we'd get out my brother's silver Honda RX 75 motorcycle and zoom it up and down the road. Or we would grab the keys to my parents' ancient dark green Cadillac and drive it through the cornfields. Once, the Cadillac ran out of gas, so we hung the keys back up and left the car there in the field, hoping our parents didn't notice. They did.

Dad continued to purchase more land and build more buildings. As he added more greenhouses to our property, my mom added two more kids to our family. When my brother Jay was born, we moved out of our trailer and into the small Cape Cod next door. The house had three tiny bedrooms and one bathroom. When my sister Michele came along three years later, we three girls crammed into one bedroom while the two boys shared another. It was crowded, but my older brother and sister and I loved our younger siblings. When they weren't on my mom's hips, they were on ours. They worked right alongside us. Every day after school, we picked in the fields or managed the store. We worked every weekend, every summer, every day except Christmas and Thanksgiving. There were times when things got so busy for my parents they would pull us out of school to help get the work done. We even worked after the shop was closed. Customers would come knock on our dining room window and ask if they could just grab a few things.

My dad only had a high school education, but when it came to growing things, he was smart. And my dad was a risk-taker. When I was in high school, he decided to build a one-acre greenhouse with specific features under one roof. The experts said it couldn't be done. But my dad did it, and several magazines recognized it as "the new state-of-the-art greenhouse."

My dad was many good things, but he had his faults. Not the least of which was that he was abusive. He had grown up in an abusive home and brought the abuse into ours. His dad sexually abused him, leaving my dad sexually deviant. Though he never molested any of his kids, his sexual perversion was poison to us. I remember being ten years old and him calling me a whore. Ten years old. I hadn't even kissed a boy.

He could be brutally mean. Explosive. He'd verbally assault my mother to the point where I'd step between them because I couldn't take it anymore. One of my dad's favorite sayings was "Women are only good for one thing, and most aren't even good at that." I grew up thinking girls should have sex so long as they made sure they were good at it.

4

I grew to hate my dad. When I was twenty, I told my husband-to-be, Steve, "If my father died today, I would walk up to his casket and spit on his face."

I hated my dad for what he did and didn't do for me and for all of us.

But even though I hated him, I didn't hate his making us work. In fact, later in my adult life I would thank him for building such a great work ethic in us. This work ethic served me well. I didn't know it back then, and my father certainly didn't intend it, but through all this, God was preparing me for his service.

God was at work. Even when I didn't know he existed, he was at work in my life. God knew what training I would need to be prepared for what he had in store for my life, for the good works he created for me before the foundation of the world (Ephesians 2:10). He knew that for me to be able to do what God asked, I'd need a big plate. I would need to be able to balance ministry, mothering, schooling, friends, extended family, cooking, cleaning.

The plate size started taking shape back on that ten-acre field. God knew I would need to bear up under some difficult things. I would need a strong back. I would need fortitude and persistence. And though my dad sinned in his abuse, God used it to teach me to be a fighter. Whether standing up to my dad when he screamed profanities at my mother or holding bushel-baskets full of wet corn while the wire handles cut into my little girl hands, I pressed on. I didn't give up. The God I didn't even know yet taught me how to live with the hard things in life. He was preparing me, and I didn't even know it.

———

God does that. I think of Moses. He was a Hebrew raised by the Pharaoh's daughter. Moses had a privileged, comfortable life. He learned under the best instructors. He had money, status, and position. And I suspect, he was raised to worship the 400-plus Egyptian gods, as any good Egyptian boy would've been. But one day, while out in the city, Moses witnessed the brutality of the Egyptians toward his Hebrew brothers and sisters. In an act of protection and rage, Moses killed the brutal Egyptian. Then, fearing for his own life, Moses ran into the desert. A desert where he would live for forty years.

I've been to that desert. It's dry—really dry. An average of only one to two inches of rain falls each year. The land is barren: no water, green plants, trees. Moses was a herdsman while living in that desert. Imagine how far he had to walk—feet filthy from the dust and sweat pouring down his brow and back—to find water and food for his sheep.

Moses lived in a desolate place, punctuated only by dirt and rock. Over those forty years he must have come to know every crevice of every rock, every corner of every mountain ridge, and every path in between. But during his forty years as a lonely, wandering, thirsty shepherd God showed up. At a burning bush, God revealed himself to Moses.

I've always marveled at how God isolated Moses. Think about it. None of the four hundred Egyptian gods were present to worship while Moses wandered the desert. Just the Great I AM, who said to Moses: "I have certainly seen the oppression of my people in Egypt. I have heard their cries of distress because of their harsh slave drivers. Yes, I am aware of their suffering. So I have come down to rescue them from the power of the Egyptians and lead them out of Egypt into their own fertile and spacious land. It is a land flowing with milk and honey—the land where the Canaanites, Hittites, Amorites, Perizzites, Hivites, and Jebusites now live. Look! The cry of the people of Israel has reached me, and I have seen how harshly the Egyptians abuse them. Now go, for I am sending you to Pharaoh. You must lead my people Israel out of Egypt" (Exodus 3:7–10).

In other words, God told Moses: "Go back and tell the most powerful man on earth, 'Hey, let all of your workforce go.'"

I get why Moses says, "Um, like, NOT!" He didn't think he could do it. And yet, Moses was exactly the man for the job. God had been preparing him, that was why he was born Hebrew but raised Egyptian. That was why he ended up in the desert in a grueling, lonely job herding sheep. God was preparing him, shaping him, and toughening him because Moses was about to fulfill "the good works God had for him" by walking God's people, one million of them, across that barren, dusty desert to the Promised Land.

Moses. God had been training him for this good work he had determined for him before the foundation of the world.

God does that.

But I didn't know that when I was twelve.

In fact, when I was growing up I didn't know any Christians, let alone God. When I was little, my quiet, calm, love-you-no-matter-what mom dragged us little kids to the Red Door Church—founded in 1887 by my great, great grandfather, Rev. James Frazier—every now and then. But we only went for a short period of time, and I was glad we stopped going. It was boring.

So I grew up with Christ and Christians as nonentities. That all changed the day I stood in a row of women "sticking" geranium cuttings in my parents' greenhouses. As I stuck the tip of the stem into the white pod filled with dirt, a woman said, "Jackie, Jesus loves you."

I rolled my eyes before turning to her. I met her smile with all the venom I could muster.

"Do you know what I think of your Jesus?" I asked. "I think Karl Marx is right; he's your opium because you can't handle real life."

She turned back to sticking her clippings. As I saw a tear roll down her cheek and watched her wipe her nose on her sleeve, I scoffed.

Typical, I thought. *Only weak people with hang-ups and/or addictions believe in Jesus.*

Those weaklings needed a fictitious god because they couldn't cope with reality. They needed a crutch. This woman was no exception. She needed Jesus as a crutch.

This view of Jesus as crutch served me well, until my friend Dean became a Christian in college. Dean was handsome. He had grown up in a good home, had good grades, and was an athlete. So I couldn't understand why he loved Jesus. Dean didn't need a crutch.

Dean and I both attended colleges near each other in North Carolina and lived near each other back home. I had the car, so I would drive us back and forth on college breaks. During those drives, I would ask questions like, "Where does the Bible say you can't swear?" And Dean would respond without judgment. He would gently respond by sharing Scriptures and talking about Jesus. Another time I asked, "Where does it say in the Bible you can't have sex before marriage?" Again he gently responded.

One Sunday morning while on college break, Dean came to my parents' home to hang out. I had been out at the bars the night before. My breath smelled like stale beer. Again I started in with my questions. Dean finally said, "Jackie, it's not how good or how bad you are. It's about whether or not you believe Jesus died on the cross for your sins. That's what gets you into heaven."

I was livid. "Are you telling me that my mother, who has lived well in an abusive marriage, who raised five kids, and gave to those in need, is going to hell simply because she doesn't believe THAT?"

"Yes," he said.

Well, that was it. I yelled for my mother in the kitchen. She came and stood in the doorway. I turned to Dean, "Tell her what you just said to me." Looking back I can't believe I put him in that position. Dean calmly repeated what he had said to my mother. She dried her hands on the dishtowel and said, "Yes, that's right, Jackie."

I was stunned. Whenever I share this story with people they wonder how I could've missed it. I've come to learn people express their faith differently. My mother is an introvert and a stoic New Englander. She doesn't talk about her faith—she lives it. I remember her taking 50-pound packages of potatoes or onions to families in need during the winter. I remember her helping the lady in the grocery store with her crying child. But mostly I remember how she loved. She had five kids, all of us different, but she let us be ourselves. And when I went through my rebellious teenager years, she still loved me. It was clear: her love for me was not based on my behavior. It just simply was. Later in my life, a professor at seminary would tell us, "If you didn't have a father who loved you, you will struggle with accepting your heavenly Father's love."

My dad was not loving. Since I "met" God, some have wondered why I haven't struggled with God's love toward me. The answer is simple: my mother. She may not have said much, but she loved more like Jesus than anyone else I know.

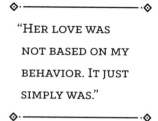

"HER LOVE WAS NOT BASED ON MY BEHAVIOR. IT JUST SIMPLY WAS."

It would be her Christ-like love and her words that day in the doorway that altered my life.

—

Because my dad was verbally abusive, I learned at a young age that words had the power to destroy.

Though this was not God's intention for words. When God spoke, there was life. "In the beginning… God said… and it was good" (Genesis 1). God spoke creation into being. In the Gospel of John, we learn Jesus is the Word. In the Book of Revelation, we see Jesus coming back with a sword in his mouth. I take that to mean he will only have to speak and war will end.

God intended words to bring life. But Satan, who isn't capable of creating anything new, misused what God created. He used words for death. In Genesis 3 he entices the woman with a lie. "'Surely you won't die,' he says. 'God knows that your eyes will be opened as soon as you eat it, and you will be like God, knowing good and evil.' The woman was convinced." (Genesis 3:4–6)

It's been that way ever since. We have a choice: words for life or death. Proverbs 18:21 says it like this, "Words kill, words give life; they're either poison or fruit—you choose" (*The Message*).

The words my mother spoke while standing in the doorway brought me life.

That evening, I lay in bed thinking about all that had been said. My dad's abuse and my own poor decisions had widened the now-oozing hole in my soul. As I lay there, I listed what I had done to try and fill that hole: drugs, drinking, boys.

I didn't know it then, but I was listing my sins. After I finished my list, I said, "Okay, Jesus, they tell me you're the answer. I don't know any other. I'll give you a shot."

I chuckle at my less-than-sound theology (as if we can give Jesus back!), but that night I had no idea. I didn't yet realize I became sealed by the Holy Spirit, forever his (Ephesians 1:13 & 4:30). I didn't realize that that night—just shy of age 22—I became a child of the King.

It's been over twenty years, and I'm still unraveling the implications of that truth in my life.

Chapter Two
NOT GOOD ENOUGHS

Duri̇ng my first two years of being a Christian, I lived much the same as I did *before* I became a Christian. Though that same year, I married the guy I had been dating for a few months. (Months! I'm sure this is why years later when Steve and I served as pastors in our church, we were never asked to work with young couples!)

As newlyweds, we made a lot of money: a six-figure income from our jobs financing cars. And we spent it—all of it. Despite (or perhaps because of) the money, those first two years of marriage were hard. Even though I loved Steve, we could not have come from more different families.

Steve grew up in an all-boy, Christian "Beaver Cleaver" home. His parents never fought—at least not in front of him. He woke in the mornings to his mother singing hymns on the piano. Communication in his family was polite, positive, and uplifting. My home, of course, had been large and loud. When my family talked, it was at a high volume. Some would call it yelling. We called it being heard.

Years later, while at marriage counseling, we learned Steve's "crisis" muscles never developed in his home. And he married me: Crisis with a capital "C." These differences clawed at our marriage. At the end of our first two years, we were nearly divorced.

We bought a VW van and hit the road. (Again perhaps why we were never asked at church to work with couples!) But we loved to travel and figured a change of scenery and pace of life couldn't hurt. While living in the van, we did a lot of questioning, sharing, and reading. That's where we conceived our first child. And it was at this time we decided it was time to "get serious about our faith," which we thought meant joining the Peace Corps.

Four months into my pregnancy, we stopped our travels and headed home to New York. Both of our extended families lived there, and this was the first grandchild to be born. We figured we could work for my parents while we took some time to figure out next steps.

After our son, Hunter, was born, Steve returned to school to get his MBA. It might have been the pressure of having a child or his disdain for greenhouse work that fueled his decision. Either way, I didn't think it was the right one.

All I knew was that whenever I read my Bible, I felt led toward seminary. I had no idea what that meant, except I was sure I didn't want to do it. So I decided to stop reading my Bible. I figured if I closed the book, I wouldn't be able to hear God.

When Steve noticed I'd stopped reading, he asked what was going on. When I told him about the call to seminary whenever I read the Word of God, Steve shocked me. He had been feeling the same call.

So Steve applied to the only seminary we knew of, Dallas Theological Seminary. The pastor who married us graduated from there, and since we liked him, we took that as an endorsement for the school.

We were both surprised when Steve got accepted. So in the summer of 1991, we packed our bags, put our one-year-old son in the back seat of our Nissan, and headed to Dallas.

We had no idea what we were heading toward. A new course of direction was being set, but we didn't even know it. I've always imagined moments like this as curtains on a stage. God pulls the curtain back just enough that we are willing to step forward. But he doesn't open them all the way. That's his grace really. Because if he pulled them *all* the way back, we would run.

Back then I had no idea what lay ahead. But what I have come to know is I have what is needed for whatever lies ahead. Jesus has already been preparing me, developing muscles I didn't even know I had—or would need. God is gracious that way. God doesn't waste anything in our lives.

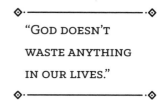

"GOD DOESN'T WASTE ANYTHING IN OUR LIVES."

—

Our first week in Dallas, we attended student orientation in a church building just off campus. We sat at round tables with other students, spouses, and an assigned professor and ate barbeque, something I had yet to develop a taste for. I sat next to a seminary student's wife and asked a question I no longer find appropriate to ask women.

"Do you have kids?" I asked.

"Yes," she said. "Five."

"Wow! Five! What are their names?"

Upon hearing that her youngest boy was named Micah, I said, "Cool name! But where on earth did you come up with that?"

Everyone at the table froze, some mid-chew, forks held at mouths. And all eyes were on me, including those of Dr. Eugene Merrill, the Old Testament professor assigned to our table. I knew I had stepped in it, but had no idea what *it* was. Later I would learn that Micah was the name of an Old Testament prophet. But this was only the beginning of realizing how little I knew.

It took only a few months of Steve coming home sharing invigorating stories from his classes for me to decide that I might as well take one of them. I had no idea how it would work out. But I figured I could l take a class or two while waiting for Steve to finish up his degree.

So, at age 26, with one child and another on the way, I applied to seminary. The application asked, "Why do you want to come to seminary?" My response? "I want to learn how to tell people about Jesus." Looking back now,

I chuckle as I imagine the person reading the application who must've wondered, "Why doesn't she just learn the wordless book[8] or read a tract?"

To my surprise, they accepted me. I started classes, one at a time.

One of the first classes was Dr. Hendricks' Hermeneutics class. When he asked us to turn to the book of Philemon, I thought he meant one of the extra books we bought at the bookstore. So I bent down into my backpack, rummaging for it until I noticed the others opening their Bibles.

I was never one of those smart students in seminary who tries to outsmart the professors. I couldn't. I was too busy asking things like, "Did you say Jesus *walked* on water?" Everyone else was pontificating on how Isaiah related to Revelation or something about Jonathan Theology. I spent the majority of my time on campus scratching my head or raising my hand. But I was a sponge trying to get to know this Jesus to whom I had entrusted my soul.

—

More than once I would scan the room of students and wonder, "What on earth am I doing here? Do they know who I am? I shouldn't be occupying one of these seats." I know I'm not the only one who has felt like this—that surely someone else deserves it more, could do it better, or would be a better fit.

In fact, that's the question thrown at the disciples when the Holy Spirit came upon them at Pentecost. In Acts 2: 1–13, the disciples start speaking in different languages. The people who heard them say, "These people are all from Galilee [read: uneducated], and yet, we hear them speaking in our own native tongue… Others in the crowd ridiculed, saying, 'They're just drunk!'"

When God uses those we don't expect—including ourselves—we question it, don't we? While we may have the wrong perspective on this, in 1 Corinthians 1:26–29, Paul steadies our doubts: "Remember, dear brothers

---

8   The wordless book is tool used to witness. The wordless book presents the salvation message using colors to represent heaven, sin, the blood of Christ, cleansing, and growth.

and sisters, that few of you were wise in the world's eyes or powerful or wealthy when God called you. Instead, God chose things the world considered foolish in order to shame those who are powerful. God chose things despised by the world; things counted as nothing at all, and used them to bring to nothing what the world considers important. As a result no one can ever boast in the presence of God."

The question isn't really about whether or not we are "good enough" to be there. It's about giving God the credit for the fact that we are.

———

It took almost eight years to graduate, mostly because I kept having kids, and mothering was a priority. I arrived in Dallas with Hunter, our one-year-old, and pregnant with my second. Hunter was twenty-months old when his brother, Hampton, was born. Then nineteen months later, I gave birth to my third child, Madison.

At twenty-eight, I had three children under the age of three-and-a-half. I attended seminary in the middle of mothering. I gave birth to Madison and was back in class the following week. (Madison came too!) I went slowly, one class per semester until Madison went to kindergarten. The pace worked for me. I had lots to learn and was still trying to figure out how Jesus walked on water. So I read all the extra reading assignments and chased rabbits down trails. I loved the stimulation at a time when my only social life was with toddlers. Besides, what was the hurry? I had no plans to go into ministry. I just wanted to get to know Jesus better.

Women frequently ask me, "When is a good time to go to seminary?" I understand their dilemma. Women give their lives to caring for so many others. They rarely consider taking time or the money from their families to equip themselves. And women struggle to justify the cost, especially since most know they might not end up with a paid position on a church staff. It seems frivolous, even luxurious. Perhaps that is one of the reasons women in the conservative evangelical world are least likely to get skilled in areas of leadership (including preaching) for the church. When women ask, I share my experience as a young mother and I tell them what my mom told me: "Jackie, if you are waiting for things to slow down, to have the time and money, it's not going to happen, so you might as well go now."

Of course, when my mother said this to me, I said, "Mom it's going to take almost eight years, and I'll be 32 when I graduate!"

Once again God used my mom to speak words of life. "Jackie," she said, "you're going to be 32 in eight years no matter what, so you might as well get the degree along the way."

I set an audacious goal. But I learned not to look at the end goal, but rather at the first small step in front of me. After that step I took the next small step. That's what it takes to get to the end of an audacious goal. As King Solomon said in Ecclesiastes 11:4, "Farmers who wait for perfect weather never plant. If they watch every cloud, they never harvest."

That's not to say it was easy. Anything worth having isn't easy. I felt like I lived in a foreign country trying to figure out this Christianity thing among weird Christians. We didn't have much money while in seminary. Steve worked three jobs and was rarely home. We had one car, which Steve had most of the time. We lived in a 900-square-foot apartment with three little ones. I was alone a lot. And in the 1990s—in the days before cell phones and Internet—I had little contact with my family back home.

I went out for my night class at DTS and to attend a Tuesday morning women's Bible study. That was it. I felt so isolated. I would walk around the apartment yelling out, "Jesus, I need a friend." And I'd hear an inner whisper: *I'm it. I'm all you've got.*

That wasn't good enough so I yelled back, "But I want a real flesh and blood friend, one who can ring my doorbell."

Again, without my knowledge, Jesus was preparing me for my future work. God had me hemmed in. In Psalm 139: 5–6, King David said, "You hem me in behind and before, and you lay your hand upon me. Such knowledge is too wonderful for me to attain."

When we hear that verse our tendency is to think, "Phew, he's got me protected on all sides." But it doesn't always translate like that. Think about it:

Hemmed in means you can't go too far to the left, or right, or front, or back. You're caged like a cat. Sometimes God does that to us. It's what he did to Moses. Moses was hemmed in that desert for forty years. That's where God had me. Except my desert was a tiny apartment filled with tiny kids.

While this situation would challenge most people, as an extrovert it was particularly hard. I love, love, love people, which means when making a decision, I seek everyone and anyone's opinion. Moving to a new place. Where to get my hair cut. Should I do public, private, or homeschooling? I'll ask everyone and anyone for advice: the grocery bagger, the woman in the elevator, my friends, whoever's around!

Jesus knew this about me, and he knew I needed to learn to go to *him* first. So he isolated me, allowed me to experience a time when he was all I had. Indeed, over time—and through a lot of yelling—I learned to seek Jesus first. To bend my ear to his voice. To this day, when faced with a decision, however big or small, I go to Jesus first. Then I go to community.

Interestingly, I still believe most Christians grow in Jesus best through community, but it's not the path Jesus had for me. Later, as my ministry life grew, I realized the value in listening to Jesus first. It helps us sift through the demanding voices in church and culture.

Learning to listen to Jesus first isn't the only benefit that came from being hemmed in. Because I was on lock-down in that tiny apartment caring for those tiny kids, I had little time on campus or in the church world. This meant I wasn't exposed to many other Christians or Christian thinking. I missed out on the theological debates on campus, including the debate on the role of women. In fact, years would pass in my education before I even knew there was a "women's issue."[9]

My first introduction to the issue was during Dr. Lucy Mabry-Foster's class, The Role of Women in the Church. She assigned the "women's issue" topic for our position papers. I didn't know it then, but I only read books and articles written from the same perspective as the seminary. At that time I would have been labeled what's known as a "received knower."

---

9   By the way, most women aren't too fond of being considered an "issue."

> "RECEIVED KNOWERS DO NOT CONSTRUCT THEIR OWN KNOWLEDGE, THEY RECEIVE IT. THEY DEPEND ON AUTHORITIES TO TELL THEM WHAT IS RIGHT OR WRONG."

In their book, *Women's Ways of Knowing*, Mary Field Belenky, Blithe McVicker Clinchy, Nancy Rule Goldberger, and Jill Mattuck Tarule conclude that most conservative evangelical women are received knowers. Received knowers do not construct their own knowledge, they receive it. They depend on authorities to tell them what is right or wrong. To a received knower there is only one right interpretation, one right answer to a problem. Ambiguity and/or paradoxes cannot be tolerated. Ideas and life are to be predictable and clearly laid out. These women would not read, attend, or participate in anything their authorities did not recommend for fear it may lead them astray. Looking back now, I see I was a received knower without knowing it. Therefore, it's not a shocker that my position paper concluded, "Women cannot teach men."

At this point my position wasn't personal, I had no dog in the fight. I had decided if I was going to do anything, it would be to teach other women the Bible. So I was safe. I wanted to teach the Bible to women because of the transformative impact women teachers had on my life. It's not to say the male professors didn't have impact—they did—but hearing a skilled woman teach biblical truth engaged me, especially as they applied the Scriptures to my female experience. I found myself in their stories.

I first heard a woman teach God's Word during a chapel at Dallas Theological Seminary. This tall, elegant woman stood up and spoke in an English accent. She used female illustrations. It was almost twenty years ago, but I still remember her sharing how she put herself in the playpen while her children roamed the house just so she could have time with Jesus.

I took this to mean that being busy with little ones was no excuse for not spending time with Jesus. Though most Christians had assured me being busy with kids was okay and normal for a young mom, that woman—Jill Briscoe—convicted me of something else by skillfully and brilliantly teaching Scriptures into my female experience. Tears rolled down my face as I listened to her speak. It was water to my female soul. It was not water to the soul for some of the male students. Many of them walked out of the chapel service in protest of a woman teaching with men present. I had no idea Christians would do this. I was perplexed—and uneasy about what this meant.

Another one of the women who impacted my life was Vicky Kraft, a straight-shooter from New York, who taught our Tuesday morning Bible study at Northwest Bible Church in Dallas. Vicky taught how Moses' mother passed down the Jewish faith to him while breastfeeding. That was what I needed: to hear God say staying home with my kids was worth it, was life-changing, was history-of-the-world-changing. My story was in Moses' story.

As the weeks went on, I marveled as Vicky's ability to take something in Hebrews and show how it related to Isaiah and then apply it to me as a woman. Sometimes she was so spot-on that I wondered if she had a camera in my tiny apartment.

After a while of sitting under God's Word with God's people, I started to change. Or more accurately, I started to become who I was. Paul said, "Therefore, if anyone is in Christ, (she) is a new creation; the old has gone, the new has come!" (2 Corinthians 5:17). This means when we put our faith in Jesus Christ, we become new, and for the rest of our lives we learn to live out that reality.

Somewhere along the way of sitting at the feet of these female teachers and learning how to live out my newness-in-Christ, I realized I wanted to teach the Bible to women. I wanted to take the Scriptures and apply them to women's everyday lives. Women who taught me truth were water to my soul, and I wanted to be that for others.

It would be a few years before I held the title "Teaching Pastor to Women." But I have to confess: if I were God and had to choose a woman to be the Teaching Pastor to Women at a conservative evangelical church in Texas, I wouldn't have picked me. I would choose a woman like Jill or Vickie. I would choose one of the smart girls in seminary who knew where Micah came from and understood how Jesus walked on water. At the very least I would choose a woman from a godly home with a solid church background. If I were God, I wouldn't choose me. But that's the thing about God—he chooses people like you and me, those who, by the world's standards, aren't *good enough*. He chooses us to accomplish his kingdom work. That's how he is assured to get the credit for what has been done.

Chapter Three

TAKING OPPORTUNITIES

M Y FIRST EXPERIENCE with serving in church on Sunday came in the form of watching potty-training two-year-olds in the nursery during the service. As a new believer, I couldn't figure out why anyone would go to church if this were required. My first opportunity to *teach* at church came in the form of standing in front of 900 kids with a pirate patch and a sword at Vacation Bible School (VBS). Suffice it to say, I didn't sign up because I loved working with kids—or playing pirate. I signed up because I wanted to be Amy's friend.

Amy and I had kids the same age, so our paths crossed as we picked our kids up from Sunday school. Amy seemed fun, and I needed a friend. Desperate and determined, I set out to become her friend by serving beside her as her co-chair for VBS. When it came time for VBS to start, we needed teachers, so I signed up. I didn't have a clue what I was doing.

But, with a treasure chest at my side, a sword in hand and a black patch over my eye, "Pirate Jack" shared the Gospel to 900 kids. No easy feat. I had to learn what big words like *propitiation, substitution,* and *restoration* even meant. In a pirate costume is probably not the way most future preachers learn these words, but the experience showed me how to think through a theological concept, break it down into digestible parts, and deliver it in an interesting way. It was there—of all places—where I sensed I was in my sweet spot. Something about it was good and right.

It showed me the importance of saying yes to the opportunities in front of you—even if it means dressing like a pirate and learning big words.

So when women who want to teach the Bible ask, "How do I get started?" my answer isn't profound. It's simply "say yes." I tell them to take the opportunities in front of them and invest in their skills. After all, that's what Jesus tells us to do in Matthew 25.

Even though it's a story from long ago, we are in it. It's about a master (that would be Jesus) and his three servants (that would be us). The master is very wealthy. He owns a lot. As the master is about to go on a trip, he calls these three men and tells them they are in charge of everything. He gives his first servant five talents, the second servant two talents and the third servant one talent. In those days a talent was worth 15 years of accumulative wages! In today's terms, if you made $50,000 a year, the Master would give you $750,000. If you made $100,000 a year, the Master would hand you $1,500,000. A lot of money—today and back then! But those servants would have lived day-to-day, so to be given even one talent would have been astronomical. Don't miss the point: these servants were given the opportunity of a lifetime (as are we).

In his book, *If You Want to Walk on Water*, John Ortberg makes three observations about this story. First: there are no no-talent people in the story. This is not a story where some are gifted and some are not. Sadly, for many of us, we think we have no talent. Jesus says not so. Let me say it again. Jesus says, NOT SO.

Second: the Master gives the talent. He decides who gets what.[10] Now this gets to us doesn't it? We women want what every other woman has: her gifting, her platform. Heck, we want her legs and her hardwood floors! Often women tell me they want to be the next Beth Moore. I want to scream back at them: "You can't be Beth Moore. She already exists!" Comparison causes

---

10   1 Corinthians 12:18

us to bury our talent. Stop trying to be like others. We need to be who we are. As one preacher put it, "Don't try to do your sermons like anyone else. That's an insult to God and all he's been doing with your 'twisted life' to prepare you for this call at this time."

> "DON'T TRY TO DO YOUR SERMONS LIKE ANYONE ELSE. THAT'S AN INSULT TO GOD AND ALL HE'S BEEN DOING WITH YOUR 'TWISTED LIFE' TO PREPARE YOU FOR THIS CALL AT THIS TIME."

Third: the amount of talents given is varied. Everyone isn't given the same amount. During one of my classes, a professor said, "God is not fair, fair meaning all things being equal. I get a large ice cream, and you get a large ice cream. God is not fair, but he is always just."

The morning after hearing this, I lined the three kids up at the table. "Guys, yesterday I learned God is not fair. But he is just. Know what this means? If God is not fair, then I don't have to be either."

Growing up, they heard that statement more than they would have liked, but I hear them repeating this now that they're adults. We don't get the same as others, but what we got was just right.[11] And we are expected to use—and to grow—what God has given us.

—

In 1994 we moved to a suburb of Dallas. We settled into our 1,400-square-foot house, found a new church down the road, and started to develop new friendships. One of my new friends, Sharon, had neighbors who wanted to know more about Jesus. Sharon asked if I would lead a Bible study in my home for these women.

Immediately, I said no. I was afraid.

Fear of failure is one reason we bury our talent. By this time, I had several years of seminary in my belt, but I was afraid they would discover I didn't know it all. What if I didn't know the answers? I was afraid of looking stupid.

---

11   John Ortberg, *If You Want to Walk on Water, You've Got to Get Out of the Boat* (Grand Rapids, Mich.: Zondervan, 2014) pp. 39–40.

Ever been there?

Not long after saying no, I sat in Sunday service, and the Holy Spirit "thunked" me. "Thunking" happens when the preacher is talking, and we hear "blah blah blah," because the Spirit has something else he wants to say.

Do you know more than they do? the Spirit asked.

Yes, I answered.

Then teach them, the Spirit said.

With trepidation I told Sharon yes.

So there I was, with six women sitting around my table eating Oreos, drinking coffee, and expectantly waiting for me to offer something profound. I was clueless. Pirate Jack was one thing, teaching adults was another. I decided the best approach would be to start where they wanted. I asked what they wanted to know, and the first thing these women asked about was Satan. They wanted to know who Satan was!

And so it went: though I prefer to teach about Jesus, my first Bible study was on Satan. Yet another lesson in just saying yes.

For the next two years, these women would gather at my table—growing together in Jesus. We worked through one wanting a breast augmentation in hopes of improving her marital sex life. Another spilled tears over the fact that she rarely extended grace to her husband. Another shared how she believed it was Tarot cards that brought her to my table. I was in over my head every time we met.

I invested hours in prep—flipping through commentaries, theological dictionaries, and books on customs and manners. My brain hurt from studying. But it takes conscious, deliberate effort to invest for Jesus. I think of those servants who had no training in investing talents. How did they gain the skill? Did they go to the local library and search the scrolls? Did they take a course on commodity trading? Did they seek out a mentor like Warren Buffet?

I find it interesting that two times in Matthew 25 the servants said, "You gave—and I did…" They understood the Master gave the talent, but it was up to them to put it to use. I wonder: do we? In the story, the Master returned to find the third man had buried his talent. The Master responded with,

"You wicked and lazy servant." Interesting choice of words: wicked and lazy. The word lazy means slothfulness. In the Old Testament, it was used to for people who let inconveniences stop them (Proverbs 6:6–9). Too often we bury our talent because we aren't educated, equipped, or skilled enough and yet, Jesus says this is lazy and wicked.

The truth about serving our Jesus is it's messy. It's difficult. It's not always "become equipped and go!" Sometimes it's "become equipped *while* going." The beauty of this is it makes you depend on Jesus. I invested time in prep and hiding behind my red and white toile recliner praying, "Lord, help me. I have no idea what I'm doing. Show up."

He showed up. He's still showing up. It's been over fifteen years since the woman who read tarot cards came to faith in our little band of women. This past month she led a team to the Congo to teach trauma healing to women! I hear the servants saying, to the Master, "You gave—I did," and I see the Master making it multiply. "The man who had received the five talents went at once," Jesus says, "and put his money to work and gained five more. So also, the one with the two talents gained two more" (Matthew 25:16–18). God gives. We put it to use. He leads a tarot card-reading woman to Congo to bring healing to women of war. Quite a return on investment of God's gifts!

———

After several years at the table, it was time for our small Bible study to leave the nest and connect to the larger Christian community. We joined the women's Bible study at Irving Bible Church under the leadership of Dr. Sue Edwards, the Pastor to Women. It wasn't long before Sue took note of our little band of women and, assuming I had the gift of teaching, asked if I would teach a message at the Bible study. When she asked, I screamed *NO* in my mind, but *yes* came out of my mouth. Only then did I learn that you don't say yes to Sue only to take it back.

Women weren't allowed to take the preaching courses at my seminary, so there I was again: unskilled and over my head. The story I had to teach was about the widow who nagged the judge to hear her case in Luke 18. I spent more than sixty hours preparing. Again with the nagging doubts. What if I didn't know the answers? What if I got up there and went blank. What if I literally fell while walking up the stairs of the stage?

I didn't sleep a wink the night before I taught. The next morning wasn't any better. I drove to church, walked into a room of several hundred women, put on the mic, and prayed like crazy: "Jesus, you've got to do something." Then I walked on stage—without tripping—and stepped up to the pulpit. Sweat rolled down everywhere: my stomach, back, and armpits. I started to speak, and the nerves were almost unbearable—for about three minutes.

Then, the Spirit showed up. He took what I had put in there and let it roll out of me. Teaching is truly a spiritual gift. That experience of sensing the Spirit's presence would be life-changing for my ministry. I would continue to build my confidence in his presence and power over the years. In the middle of the message, I used my personal story to illustrate a point. I shared about my abusive dad and how I took his sin and added mine upon it. I told about my wild-child, sex–drugs–and–rock-n-roll past and about the devil tattoo on my hip (always interesting at seminary pool parties!). My personal story explained, proved, applied, and restated the point in the passage. God's grace, mercy, and power were on display. I could sense the transformative work of the Spirit moving in the room.

I didn't know at the time that Sue was in the back cringing. (I never knew she reacted that way until years later when I read it in one of her books!) She also noted that my honesty opened the floodgates for authenticity among our women. I wasn't shooting for that. I was just doing what I learned in my family: you talk about everything. Perhaps it's a lime green thing. Looking back, I'm grateful Sue never frowned upon my style of teaching. If she had, I probably would have shrunk back from my calling. I wonder if the servants had people like Sue in their lives. I know it's what enabled me to invest my talent.

—

Shortly after my first "grown-up" teaching experience, I was asked to speak at a small women's retreat in Louisiana. I was pumped. I drove three hours, taught four sessions to 35 women, and got paid $100. I loved every minute of it. Hanging with those women, hearing their stories, listening to their hopes, praying over their pain, I was in my sweet spot. Tears rolled down my cheeks when I said goodbye and headed down Route 20 to Dallas. That day in the car, I knew: I was made to teach. In the movie the *Chariots of Fire*, Eric Liddell says, "I believe God made me for a purpose, but he also made me fast. And when I run I feel His pleasure." That's what I felt: this gut level, Spirit-assured kind of thing. Whether we believe it or not, God gives each of us moments like this.

The Apostle Paul said, "Yet when I preach the gospel, I cannot boast, for I am compelled[12] to preach. Woe to me if I do not preach the gospel!" (1 Corinthians 9:16). I felt the same. There was no going back. I put a stake in the ground. I had said yes—to kids at VBS, to neighbors wanting to study the Bible, to a lecture, to a retreat—and discovered I was called to teach and preach the Word of God to women… or so I thought.

—

Of course, there's a cost to saying yes.

There have been times I've wondered if saying yes was worth it.

As I neared the end of my seminary years, I increased my work under Sue's ministry. As a volunteer, I taught, wrote curriculum, and trained other women to teach. I also spoke at conferences ten weekends out of the year, a number our family decided together was appropriate for us. While this may seem strange to some, our kids always had a say in our vocation.

As much as I believe in saying yes to the Spirit and to what is before me, I also know that to stay married and have kids who don't resent Jesus means having to say no—a lot. No to baking cookies for my son's fifth-grade class.

---

12   To be "compelled" to preach means to be driven onward by an irresistible and undeniable compulsion to do so.

No to lunches with friends or evenings playing Bunco. No to decorating our new home or getting a manicure. No to hobbies, movies, or reading for fun. I even limited my haircuts to twice a year.

Saying yes to Jesus comes at a cost. And yet, even the costs come with blessings. For instance, I realized that I could keep my schedule highly disciplined and focused because of what my dad had taught me. So, where once I had struggled to find an appropriate Father's Day card (most being filled with mushy gushy stuff about dads that just didn't hold true for me), now I was able to write my dad a sincere thank-you note. He instilled a great work ethic in me. I knew how to do hard work. I had learned it in that field. My dad had prepared me for ministry.

The three servants in our story basically won the lottery. They could do whatever they wanted. Go wherever they wanted. Buy whatever they wanted. We can almost hear their giddy pillow talk at night: "Oh sweetie pie, let's get you a new car! Let's go to Greece. You've always wanted to go to Greece." It had to be hard to forgo all this and head to the library to read scrolls on commodity trading. Just as we can be *lazy* by letting inconveniences stop us from fulfilling our purpose, so can we be lazy by letting *con*veniences stop us. There is an abundance of ways we can get sidetracked down life's hallways and forget our purpose of investing for our Master.

One Saturday afternoon, as we lingered by the pool, a friend said, "With all your work, school, and travel, someone must be paying a price."

Her inference was that either my kids or my marriage must be suffering. Yes, my kids and husband made sacrifices for my calling (as I did for theirs). But the person who paid the price was me. I woke before dawn to get a run in before the family morning routine. I squeezed in homework and teaching prep during the kids' naptimes or after their bedtime. Later when the kids went to elementary school, I used every minute to work. When they were home, I was present. When their friends came to play, I did more homework—right smack in the middle of the house where everyone was playing. Growing up in that small 1,100-square-foot Cape Cod house with all those people and farm help coming and going was God's way of preparing me for this, and I didn't even know it.

Like most working moms, every minute was accounted for. I tried to find books to help maximize time, but it turned out I was already doing what they prescribed. One of the most helpful pieces of advice I received was from a woman who had already walked in my shoes. Jill Briscoe (the Englishwoman from seminary chapel) is a preacher, wife, mother, grandmother, author, radio host, etc. I had the opportunity to ask her how she and her husband balanced their ministry lives. In my world, I had learned priorities go as such: God, Husband, Kids, Work. A list. But Jill spoke of a circle.

"Every morning I wake and ask Jesus 'Which family today, Lord?'" she says.

There are ah-ha moments in life and this was one of them. I got out a napkin and drew a circle—more like a spoke wheel with God in the center and everyone else on a spoke. It made sense. It meant reliance on Jesus every day—all day. And when I thought about it, we really don't live the list. Who puts their husband first when their kid is upstairs puking all night long? I've been living in a circle ever since.

And then there's the friend thing. Growing up I always had friends, many friends—always several best friends. My mother used to tell me I was fortunate to have so many close friends. She said most people didn't have that many deep friendships in their whole lifetime. But when I started teaching, friendships got complicated. In the megachurch model, there's a tendency to idolize our church leaders, and it took work to bridge the gap created by others thinking I was so "spiritual." I mean who wants to be near one of those people?

Once I was in Walmart with my three kids getting school supplies. A woman approached to inform me she'd been observing us throughout the store. She wanted to see if how I lived off stage reflected my persona on stage. Now I was freaking out. That's called *stalking!* And for the first time in my life, I had to be leery of women who wanted to be my friend solely because of my or my husband's position in the church (Steve was the Executive Pastor at Irving Bible Church). They figured if they were near me, they would have influence in the inner circle of leadership. Ugh.

And then there was this unspoken, subtle competition and comparison that happens among church women. Of course, this happens with all women, but takes a unique form when it's cloaked in Christianity, especially as some of our church teachings have fueled the competition and comparison. Consider the mixed messages we offer about what it means to be the "ideal" biblical (light pink) woman. Women today have choices about marriage, childrearing, and lifestyle, and our teachings about the "ideal" woman cause confusion, insecurity, and competition. Is it okay for a woman to work while having kids or is a stay-at-home mom more "ideal?" Is it okay for our kid to go to public school or is it more "ideal" to put them in a Christian school? And what do we do with single women and those married without children? Because underneath we are all wondering if we are measuring up. We walk around with a layer of insecurity, guilt, and self–doubt. We look at other women and think, *If she represents the "ideal" biblical woman then who am I?* Or, *Is it okay to be lime green in a light pink world?* We face judgment for our choices: from society, the church, each other, and from ourselves.

When Jesus said, "follow me" he wasn't doing a cattle call. Not everyone walks the same path. Every life is unique. God was leading and choosing to use my life in ways that were not predicated by how he worked in most other women's lives (and vice versa). In this way, the path he was choosing for my life was costly to my friendships, as it was hard to relate and connect with the women around me whose paths were quite different.

It's well documented that working moms struggle with guilt about failing their kids. For me, the guilt-struggle was spiritual. I didn't want my kids to resent Jesus because of my work. To teach other women about Jesus, yet fail my kids, was not an option.

In 1994 a team of us women were invited to teach at a women's conference in Kilgali, Rwanda. It was right after the genocide, and things were still uneasy in the country. The night before our departure, with everyone else in bed, I cried out in fear from the couch: "Lord, will I come home?"

No answer.

I asked again.

No answer.

I started to bargain with God, as we do: "God you do know that kids don't fare well without their mothers. They won't like you if you take me away."

Then I heard his gentle voice: *Jackie, don't you think I can parent your children?*

◇————◇
"HE LOVED
LAUNCHING HIS
WIFE INTO HER FULL
CALLING."
◇————◇

Not what I wanted to hear. I wrestled with God that night. God wanted to know if I *really* trusted him, and the proof was whether or not I would entrust my children to him. It wouldn't be the last time he asked.

Every decision to speak, travel, teach, or attend school stirred up a fear that this would be the one thing that tipped the scale for my kids. Truth is, I probably would have let that fear stop me from pursuing God's purpose without my husband Steve. He wouldn't have it. He encouraged, supported, and many times, pushed me to places I didn't want to go.

In her book *Lean In*, Sheryl Sandberg says, "I truly believe that the single most important career decision a woman makes is whether she will have a life partner and who that partner is. I don't know a woman in a leadership position whose life partner is not fully—and I mean fully—supportive of her career."

I couldn't agree more.

Sandberg goes on to say, "Contrary to the popular notion that only unmarried women can make it to the top, the majority of the most successful female business leaders have partners … Not surprising, a lack of spousal support can have the opposite effect on a career. In a 2007 study of well-educated professional women who had left the paid workforce, 60% cited their husbands as a critical factor in their decision. These women specifically listed their husbands' lack of participation in child care and other domestic tasks … as reasons for quitting."[13]

---

13   Sandberg, Sheryl, *Lean In* (New York: Alfred A. Knopf, 2013) p. 110

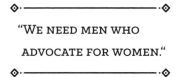

"WE NEED MEN WHO ADVOCATE FOR WOMEN."

Steve has been a full partner: he cleaned, cooked, and cared for the kids—without griping. He did it because he loved launching his wife into her full calling. When I returned home from a conference, the house was clean, kids well cared-for, flowers on the table, and dinner in the oven. We would sit around the table catching up on everyone's weekend, and eventually Steve would turn to me and say, "Jackie, tell the kids what God did through you this weekend." I shared a story or two about women's lives being moved from death to life.

We women need men like Steve in our lives. Whether it's in the home or the workplace, we need men who advocate for women.

———

In Matthew 25:16–21, the Master returned to settle accounts with the servants. (That means Jesus is coming back—Woohoo!)

The man who had received five bags of gold brought the other five. 'Master,' he said, 'you entrusted me with five bags of gold. See, I have gained five more.' His master replied, 'Well done, good and faithful servant! You have been faithful with a few things; I will put you in charge of many things. Come and share your master's happiness!' The man with two bags of gold also came. 'Master,' he said, 'you entrusted me with two bags of gold; see, I have gained two more.' His master replied, 'Well done, good and faithful servant! You have been faithful with a few things; I will put you in charge of many things. Come and share your master's happiness!'

We're in this story. One of the talents God gave me was the spiritual gift of teaching. I have tried to invest that gift as diligently as I could. And I have seen the dividends it yields. Problem was, I stopped reading after that part of the verse. But it continues, "You have been faithful with a few things; I will put you in charge of many things."

It may sound silly, but it never occurred to me that there would be more. I was good with where I was. I wanted to stop there.

But God. Whenever you read "but God" in the Scriptures, something is about to change. I was about to be thrown in the limelight of the debate over the role of women. It was a topic I had avoided like the black plague. Every time anyone brought it up, I thought, "I'm not going there for anything." I was content with where I was. I loved teaching women. It wasn't my battle. Or so I thought. Truth is, I was afraid. I knew the issue was explosive, and no one wants to get blown up. Dr. Scot McKnight wrote, "The subtle decision I regret is that, because the issues [debate about the women in church ministries] around TEDS [Trinity Evangelical Divinity School] were so inflammatory and anyone who thought otherwise [other than interpretation of gender restrictive texts] was held either as theologically liberal or intellectually suspect, I made the decision not to enter into the public debate."[14]

McKnight is not the only one who confessed to fear of being blown up. One pastor shared, "To be completely truthful, I am now convinced that what I deeply feared during my early years in the ministry was rejection. I desperately wanted to be a successful pastor (who doesn't?). I served among all male pastors who held the same view [on the women's issues] putting myself in a most difficult position. This could cost me my ministry. I had a young family to support."[15]

Fear will bury our talent.

Saying yes will always be costly.

---

14   Scot McKnight, *Blue Parakeet* (Grand Rapids, Mich: Zondervan, 2008) p. 146.

15   Alan F. Johnson and Dallas Willard, *How I Changed My Mind About Women In Leadership* (Grand Rapids, Mich: Zondervan, 2010) p. 23.

Chapter Four
INVISIBLE TRIP WIRES

I DON'T KNOW EXACTLY when I changed. It wasn't a paint-by-numbers kind of process, but more like watercolor. However, somewhere along the way, I became convinced women could preach from the pulpit.

One of the paint strokes took place while I spoke at a retreat center in Upstate New York. At one of the lunch breaks, two women at our table brought up the topic of submission. Their views were not mine, but I stayed quiet. As they proceeded to share their views, the woman to my right lowered her head. I knew—at least I thought I knew—what it meant. She excused herself. As she walked away I prayed, *Lord, give me an opportunity to talk with her.* After lunch I headed back to my room when I saw the woman standing next to the very door I was heading towards. (*Love it when you do that, Jesus!*)

Timidly she said, "Can I ask you something?"

"Of course."

She proceeded to tell how she homeschooled her four children, all under the age of twelve, and how her husband had been physically abusive so she separated for a time. They were back together now.

I interrupted, "Did the abuse stop?"

I already knew the answer by the way she hung her head in shame.

◈·————————————·◈

"HOW WE INTERPRET
SCRIPTURE CAN BE
HARMFUL AND SOMETIMES
DOWNRIGHT DANGEROUS
FOR WOMEN."

◈·————————————·◈

She responded, "Well, it's better than it was."

My heart sank.

She continued. Her twelve-year-old had started to act up and she was concerned it was her fault.

"In what way?" I asked.

"The women at church said he's acting up because when I separated I wasn't being submissive."

She referenced Exodus 34:7, "The sins of the father are passed down…" These women had used Scripture to put an iron collar on this woman's neck.

More and more I began to run into women (and men) for whom Scripture had been used as a weapon. It became apparent that how we interpreted Scripture could be harmful and sometimes downright dangerous for women (and men).

Another stroke on the canvas came when I cleaned under my bed. I have a philosophy: "You don't have to clean what you don't see." So since I couldn't see under the bed, it hadn't been cleaned in years. But when I finally looked, I saw dust-balls, hair bands, paper clips. And now that I'd seen it, I had to clean it. Having assessed the situation, I realized to accomplish the job I would need to move the furniture. I pushed. Pulled. Shimmied. Nothing moved. So I sat on the floor, back against the wall, and pushed with my legs. There was a sharp snap. *Must have pulled a muscle in my back,* I thought.

The next day the kids, Steve and I loaded our maroon Suburban and drove to Oneonta, N.Y.

Spending summer in upstate New York was a family tradition, as was reading books on the bestseller list. Prior to our drive north I had read *The Secret Life of Bees* by Sue Monk Kidd and loved it. So I grabbed her second book thinking I would enjoy that too. I didn't. In fact I was frustrated by her inference that the early church worshiped goddesses. She said there was proof. I emailed my professors; I wanted to know how to locate such said "proof." I ordered every book I could find on women in the church. I threw them in my white laundry basket; Steve loaded them in our Suburban for our summer in New York. I was done with reading for fun. I was on a hunt for truth.

By the time we arrived at my mom's I was in deep pain, but I refused to see a doctor until we returned to Dallas. I kept thinking, "Oh it will get better." I spent my summer on my mother's living room couch. Reading. Until the laundry basket was empty. My head was so full I thought it would explode.

That summer, I learned about the two "camps" when it comes to women's roles in the church: complementarians and egalitarians. Think Republican and Democrat. Complementarians believe that while women are equal to men in essence (value) they are different in function (role). They argue by God's created design man and woman form a complementary relationship, one enhancing the role of the other. Men serve as the "head" or leader in the home and church, while women are to serve as helpers in submissive assistance to men. The created design was disrupted at the fall which brought about woman's desire to rule over her husband and in return resulted in his ruling over her with power and strength (at his worst state being abuse). Through Christ's redemption those relationships are restored to their original created design. Because of Christ, men and women can live as intended in the original design, men as servant leaders while women respond in submission to his leadership. There are six gender-restricted texts used to support the complementarian position: Genesis 1–3; 1 Corinthians 11:1–16; 1 Corinthians 14:33–36; 1 Timothy 2:8–15; Ephesians 5:21–33; and 1 Peter 3:7.

The egalitarians—the second camp—believe that prior to the fall both women and men were equal in essence (value) and function (role). They argue it is illogical to say women are equal in essence but not in function. They believe at the fall the equality between man and woman was disrupted. Now instead of both having dominion over earth their dominion is turned into domination between and toward each other (the genders). Egalitarians use the life and teachings of Jesus to support their position of equality. Their argument hinges on six passages: Genesis 1:26–27; Genesis 2:18; Genesis 2:22–24; Galatians 3:28; 1 Corinthians 11:11–12; and 1 Corinthians 12:7–11.

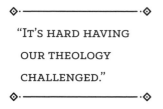
My seminary camped with the complementarians. Somehow while walking around the campus I caught their position, which is why I said no when asked by a church leader to teach a mixed Sunday school class. But there I was on my mother's couch being challenged by this second camp, the egalitarian position. *What if I'm being led astray?* I worried. After all, at seminary, I had learned that those who held the egalitarian view were either theologically liberal or intellectually suspect.

Throughout the summer, I cried out to Jesus, *Lord, I want to be faithful. Don't let me go astray.* It's hard having our theology challenged.

One thing became apparent by the end of the summer: I had made a decision on where I stood, as a complementarian, without having all the information. I hadn't been given the whole story. It wasn't a particular person's argument that caused the shift so much as a preponderance of evidence that demanded it.

It may seem elementary, but I was surprised to learn that history and culture are as important in interpreting a passage as the language. Information such as: prior to 313 AD, the church met in homes where women could lead. However, when Constantine declared Christianity the dominant religion of the Roman Empire, church became a public affair, a place where women were restricted. That piece of history shapes my lens when reading passages on church leadership.

Then there was the controversial passage in 1 Timothy 2. Paul wrote to Timothy because he was concerned for the Ephesians to come to truth (1 Timothy 1:10–11, 2:4, 2:5[16]). In Ephesus the goddess cult Artemis exalted females and considered them superior to males. Paul instructed women (most likely women who came out of the Artemis cult) to be quiet and learn. Paul's statement was radical since women weren't allowed to study the Torah.

---

16   For there is one God and one mediator between God and mankind, the man Christ Jesus, who gave himself as a ransom for all people. 1 Timothy 1:5–6.

Yet, he breaks with culture. Then Paul used the creation argument as reason for his previous instruction.[17] One theologian argued that Paul was concerned about the misunderstanding of the Gospel. (This sounds like Paul to me. He's always about the Gospel!) The logic went like this: The first man on Earth was a man, not a woman. If we say the first person was a woman, we lose the parallel between the "first man" who is "earthly" and the "second man," Jesus Christ, who is "from heaven" (1 Corinthians 15: 46–47). Paul would not be okay with them missing the Messiah by expecting a woman and missing "the man Christ Jesus."

Then, of course, there's that ever so clear (not!) verse "and women will be saved by childbirth."[18] I'm still figuring that one out, but that speaks to my point. That summer, I learned the Scriptures weren't always all that clear, that to bring clarity we must understand the culture. These ideas—among many others—put cracks in my previous picture.

Somewhere along the way I "caught" that egalitarians were liberal, that they were fast and loose with Scripture. On the couch, I learned not so. The theologians represented in both camps loved Jesus Christ and held to a high view (authority) of Scripture; both fit within orthodoxy.[19] The main difference between these two camps was they differed on their conclusions. The true difference was they didn't agree on the non-essentials.[20]

And then there was the discovery that many of our church fathers were misogynists! It became apparent our church fathers' interpretations of passages like 1 Timothy 2 were influenced by their low view of women. For

---

17   For Adam was formed first, then Eve. And Adam was not the one deceived; it was the woman who was deceived and became a sinner. 1 Timothy 2:13–14

18   1 Timothy 2:15

19   "Heresy is not located in one's beliefs about baptism, the continuation of certain spiritual gifts, women in ministry, or political issues. It is a specific and direct denial of any of the central beliefs of the Christian church about the deity and identity of the triune God and about the person and work of Jesus Christ." rachelheldevans.com/blog/heresy-justin-holcomb May, 21 2014.

20   Footnote: Theologians in the same camp also differ with each other. I had two professors from the same seminary conclude very differently on the issue of divorce.

example, Tertullian (A.D. 160 – 220) believed women were more easily deceived; that we are more vulnerable to false teaching.

"Do you not know that each of you is an Eve?" Tertullian wrote. "You are the devil's gateway... You are the first deserter of the divine law: you are she who persuaded him whom the devil was not valiant enough to attack. You destroyed so easily God's image, man. On account of your desert—that is, death—even the Son of God had to die."[21]

Another church father, John Chrysostom (A.D. 380), assessed Eve's deception—and women's nature—in terms of a victory of the weaker over the stronger. Eve's deception was worse than Adam's, because she was deceived by an inferior and subordinate animal, whereas Adam was persuaded by an equal, and he was not captivated by appetite. In turn, Chrysostom asserts that Eve's character is representative of the whole female sex: women, collectively, are weak and fickle. [22]

In thinking about the sexes, the Fourth Century church father, Augustine (A.D. 380) identified woman with the temporal world and man with the spiritual. He asserted that "the woman herself alone" is not the image of God. Man is, woman is not. When Augustine considered what makes a man the image of God, his answer was: man's mind. Augustine concluded that man's mind was more naturally inclined to contemplate higher things, whereas women's heads are filled with thoughts of "lower things." Therefore, women should keep their heads covered: "woman should be required to cover her brain." He also believed God did not create the woman for any other reason than procreation. Augustine writes:

> *If it were not the case that the woman was created to be man's helper*
> *specifically for the production of children, then why would she have been*
> *created as a "helper"? Was it so that she might work the land with him?*
> *No because there did not yet exist any such labor for which he needed*
> *a helper, and even if such work had been required, a male would have*

---

21   Tertullian, "On the Apparel of Women," p. 14.

22   Chrysostom, "Homily 9," p. 435–6.

*made a better assistant. One can also posit that the reason for her cre-
ation as a helper had to do with the companionship she could provide
for the man, if perhaps he got bored with his solitude. Yet for company
and conversation, how much more agreeable it is for two male friends to
dwell together than for a man and a woman! I cannot think of any reason for woman's being made as a man's helper, if we dismiss the reason
to procreation.*[23]

I belly laughed at Saint Thomas Aquinas' (1225 – 1274) teachings that "women are dominated by their sexual appetite and that men are ruled by reason." Yup—all the years working in the church I noticed a trend: men complaining that their wives always wanted sex while they just want to reason! I'd say there's been a theological shift since Aquinas' day, wouldn't you?[24]

When these men painted their interpretations into church history, they did so wearing misogynist glasses. Much of our theology today is built off their foundation. Knowing their low view of women should make us question the influence of their teachings on interpretations today. There's humility in admitting we see Scripture through our cultural lens and sometimes we just might not have gotten it right.[25] As Jane Austen said, "Seldom, very seldom, does complete truth belong to any human disclosure; seldom can it happen that something is not a little disguised, or a little mistaken."[26] There are legitimate reasons to question, re-examine and at times change our theological position.

---

23   Sarah Sumner, *Men and Women in the Church* (Downers Grove, Ill.: InterVarsity Press, 2003) p. 59–61.

24   "Church tradition should always be taken seriously and should never be ignored but sometimes it needs to be corrected or rejected." Kevin Giles, *The Trinity & Subordination* (Downers Grove, Ill.: InterVarsity Press, 2002) p 5.

25   "Christians should agree that there exists a perfect orthodoxy in the mind of God; however, the proliferation of schisms, disagreements, and divisions throughout church history points to the fact that we as sinful and fallible humans are imperfect at agreeing precisely on that orthodoxy." rachelheldevans.com/blog/heresy-justin-holcomb, May 21 2014.

26   www.literaturepage.com/read/emma-392.html, March 23 2015.

That's what happened in the 1600s when Christians believed the sun revolved around the earth—ideas supported by verses such as 1 Chronicles 16:30, Psalm 104:5, and Joshua 10:13. Galileo's belief that the earth revolved around the sun got him condemned as a heretic. Not until 1979 did Pope John Paul admit the Catholic Church erred in its treatment of Galileo. We aren't all-knowing. We aren't always right. It was true of our church fathers. It was true of Galileo's prosecutors in the 1600s. It was true in the Eighteenth Century (over slavery). And it may be true about the role of women in the Twenty-First Century.

—

We loaded the Suburban with suitcases, blankets, toys and treats and headed back to Dallas. On the drive I realized I felt cheated. A bit angry. *Why wasn't I trusted with both sides of this story?*

Many of us have experienced this—where we "bought" something we were told in church to find out later it wasn't quite right—or right enough. We feel cheated, don't we? That's where I was when we rolled into Dallas with an aching back and a sad heart.

The next day at the doctor, I learned I did not have a pulled a muscle but rather two cracked bones in my lower back. The doctor surmised the breaks were a result of a childhood impact on the back. Hmm. I had to wonder if it was all that bending and planting. Where I discovered some parts of my childhood had prepared me specifically for my life in ministry, I also realized some things from my past needed to break before I could heal and take next steps. By the end of that summer, things that had confused me began to make sense, things that had been cloudy were becoming clear.

—

In the fall of 2002, Sue Edwards stepped down from her position as Pastor to Women at Irving Bible Church. The following January I found myself on staff as the new Teaching Pastor to Women. I reported to Julie, the new Directional Leader of Women's Ministry. Unlike most women's ministry positions, my job consisted solely of shepherding, teaching, writing, and training other women to do the same.

As far as I know, I was the only conservative evangelical woman in the country with my title and position. It wasn't rocket science to surmise from my hire that significant changes were occurring on our leadership team. As the Executive Pastor (who was also my husband) stated, "We were going through this process as a leadership team. When I got there, all the lead pastors were men, except for the children's pastor, who was quiet and quaint and nice. I just felt like we were missing out on a heck of a lot of good talent, and a lot of good interaction, from a leadership point of view, by not having women in leadership. So we slowly but surely were on that track, which created some issues..."

It created some issues all right! As we women moved into traditionally male space we bumped into gender lines. Lines no one was even aware we had. I call them invisible trip wires. We didn't know they were there until someone tripped over it.

One of the issues was (and still is in many places) awkwardness. The idea of women in leadership makes many people *uncomfortable.* Just as when someone gets in an elevator and continues to talk on their phones or doesn't turn to face the doors. Or if someone comes over for dinner and walks straight into your bedroom, plops down and starts talking. It's uncomfortable because it breaks social norms; norms we can't always articulate until they are broken.

That's exactly what Mary did in Luke 10:38–42.[27] Martha is busy preparing a meal while Mary "sat at the Lord's feet listening to what he said" (10:39 NIV). Martha, exasperated because Mary is not helping in the kitchen, demands that Jesus instruct Mary to help. Jesus responds to Martha,

---

27 "As Jesus and the disciples continued on their way to Jerusalem, they came to a certain village where a woman named Martha welcomed him into her home. Her sister, Mary, sat at the Lord's feet, listening to what he taught. But Martha was distracted by the big dinner she was preparing. She came to Jesus and said, "Lord, doesn't it seem unfair to you that my sister just sits here while I do all the work? Tell her to come and help me." But the Lord said to her, "My dear Martha, you are worried and upset over all these details! There is only one thing worth being concerned about. Mary has discovered it, and it will not be taken away from her." *Luke 10: 38–42*

"Only one thing is needed. Mary has chosen what is better, and it will not be taken away from her" (Luke 10:42 NIV).

A common modern interpretation of this text is that it stresses the importance of having a quiet time, of "sitting with Jesus." But to fully understand what Jesus is communicating here, we have to appreciate the cultural significance of Mary's posture. For a First-Century Jew or other ancient person, sitting at someone's feet would be a highly symbolic act. It would acknowledge the other person's higher education. For example, rabbinic students would typically sit at their rabbi's feet as a way of expressing respect to the rabbi. Describing his own rabbinical learning, the Apostle Paul says, "I am indeed a Jew... brought up in this city [Jerusalem] *at the feet of Gamaliel,* taught according to the strictness of our fathers' law" (Acts 22:3 NKJV, emphasis added).

What rabbinic students hoped to get from their rabbi was a deep understanding of the Torah and the Law. This education was considered the highest form of learning in Judaism. And yes, a rabbi's disciple was expected to learn in quietness and full submission. If all went according to plan, the end result would be that the student (disciple) would know all that his rabbi knew about the Torah and the Law.

What is striking about the story from Luke is that, in First-Century Judaism, women were excluded from this kind of learning. Yet here is Mary, adopting the posture of the disciple. She is learning at the feet of her rabbi. Considering the culture, that's radical. Just as radical is Jesus' response to Martha. In essence, what Jesus tells Martha is what Paul will later teach Timothy: "A woman should learn" (1 Timothy 2:11 NIV). Culturally, she might be excluded from this higher level of learning—but Jesus didn't exclude her. In other words, Jesus welcomed the light pink *and* the lime green (and soft yellow and bright purple and...) women.

And where did all this take place? In male space. Ancient Near Eastern culture drew distinctions between public space and private space. Public space was male space. Rabbis taught in the public space. A father, brother, or husband considered a woman sexually promiscuous if she roamed in public space unaccompanied. We see reminders of this even today, in Islamic cultures. And the distinction applied even within the home. Although generally the home was considered private space, even inside the home there were areas set aside as public space—for the males—and private space for the family as a whole, including the females. Martha was cooking and Mary was in the living room—a *male space*. Think about who was with her. Jesus and the disciples—*men*. Can you see the disciples' wiggling body language as they shot glances at each other. "Doesn't Jesus know she's not supposed to be in here?" Apparently Mary was willing to cross any and all cultural boundaries to follow Jesus. Apparently she knew that this was an opportunity of a lifetime. And regardless of the looks of disgust and the angry stares she was going for it. Jesus said, "Mary has chosen the one thing and it will not be taken from her."

I sat in a room with stares and glares too. Pastoral staff meetings were every Monday at noon in the computer room at church. The first day I walked in, pastors were seated at the eight tables put in a square formation eating the lunch Donna, my husband's admin, had provided. We joked and laughed as we passed dessert, the big red bowl of assorted candy. Finally seriousness settled in, and we got to work. A conversation ensued between two pastors with strong personalities (you might call them bright red!)—both were known to be snarky men who could verbally put you in your place. I felt right at home. Until, that is, I heard myself say—out loud—what was in my mind.

"That's not right," I said to the snarky men. "I don't agree at all!"

The heated debate came to a screeching halt. Heads tilted, eyes stared, expressions asked, *Huh?*

We all knew something had happened. I had crossed this norm of what a Christian woman, particularly a southern Christian woman was like. In culture and the church we have taught gendered (God-designed) characteristics.[28] We've been informed that men are rational, analytical, brave, competitive, and *assertive* whereas women are nurturing, compassionate and they are

---

28   We are not androgynous. There are differences between the genders, but I suspect those differences are not as vast as we've been taught. It's just not true that men are from Mars and women are from Venus. We are from Earth. It behooves us to remember what Dorothy Sayers, a contemporary of C.S. Lewis, said: "Women are more like men than any other creature."

supposed to be "gentle and quiet." (We have specific pictures of what 1 Peter 3:3–4 meant by gentle and quiet, and it does not include assertiveness.) My female assertive voice roused their ideals about gender. It took a few seconds, but then we all recovered. After all, we knew each other. We already had an incarnational relationship, something that would become a driving force for change in our church.

Churches have different structures for the Sunday pulpit preaching, IBC's form was an all-male preaching team that shared the pulpit responsibilities. The team met periodically to discuss the different interpretations, theological bents and Scripture exegesis for the upcoming series. I was the first woman to join their all-male team. A few meetings in, I challenged one of the guys' interpretations of a passage. There was that look again, the tilted head, the *huh?* look that signified Augustine's legacy still lingered in our church.

The message—whether they realized it or not (and most of them didn't)—was that they expected women to be "less than" when it came to Scripture, doctrine, and theology. There was a quick recovery. It wouldn't take long before the men welcomed my perspective, mind, and presence. Down the line, while on the golf course, my senior pastor would be asked by a fellow senior pastor whom he trusted with his pulpit.

His reply? "Jackie." Now it was his turn to get the stares and glares! I have a deep gratitude for him. It takes a secure man to invite a woman to shine in her gifting, especially when her gifting is preaching.

———

No boy wants to be beat out by a girl. I learned that on the playground in elementary school. I was one of the best kickball players in our school. I could make that red rubber ball sail in the sky. (Allow me to brag: It was the only sport I was ever good at!) That's when I learned boys don't like to be one-upped by a girl. We raise our boys to abhor being called a girl or sissy.[29]

---

29   Don McPherson, a quarterback in the NFL and Canadian football league, states, "*We don't raise boys to be men, we raise them not to be women.*" Check out his work on reconstructing masculinity: www.donaldmcpherson.com/qa.html

That teaching continues to plague men and women in the boardroom and the church. Listen to how one female theologian was advised: "When I was a student at Trinity, one of my professors called me into his office and said to me in a warm, fatherly tone, 'Sarah, do not show the full color of your plume; it will intimidate the men.' My professor sincerely believed he was doing me a favor by telling me not to express myself without also holding back. He liked me, and he didn't want me to become controversial or lose the good favor of the men."[30] Can you hear the fear? *What if she outshines me?* The message we women receive is be less so he thinks he's more. This feels like manipulation, doesn't it?

When Sue Edwards left her position as Pastor to Women at IBC, she left Julie and me with a well-established women's Bible study. At one time we had seven teachers on the teaching team, we were writing and publishing curriculum and we had over sixty table leaders and nine hundred women attending. There was a buzz among our women and they shared their excitement with their husbands. Women started asking if their husband's could attend the study too. I wasn't keen on the idea. In the conservative evangelical world, women are less apt to speak up about theology and Bible when men are present. I longed for women to be empowered by hearing themselves talk about Jesus and Scripture.

But I knew trouble was brewing when men started harassing our men's pastor: "Why isn't our study as good as the women's?" Nothing good comes out of questions like that. I knew men don't like to be upped one by women, so I scheduled a dinner to discuss the issue. My colleague was "man enough" to admit the comparison had been difficult for him. I felt anger that my brother had been belittled like a kid being teased on the playground. It should not be this way. I shouldn't have to be less so he can feel more nor should he feel less because a woman was succeeding.

---

30   Sarah Sumner, *Men and Women in the Church* (Downers Grove, Ill.: InterVarsity Press, 2003) p. 27.

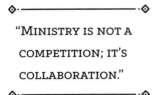

Ministry is not a competition; it's collaboration. Too many people need Jesus for us to spend time on sibling rivalry. We need everyone in the battle using everything they've got right where they are to advance the kingdom.

Of course, the idea of men and women working together also leads to the sex thing.[31] The movie *When Harry Met Sally* asked the age-old question, "Can men and women be friends or does the sex thing always get in the way?" It seems the church has answered with a big fat *yes*: sex always gets in the way. The church's narrative is one of romance and danger. Women tempt men, whether they intend it or not, and men by nature are lascivious (which is opposite of St. Aquinas' teachings). We hear this message all the time.

At a luncheon hosted for a group of female seminary graduates, the question was asked, "How could we better equip women for ministry?" Our answer was to teach women how to work with male leadership. Quickly our hosts responded with a reminder of perils of infidelity in the church.

There it was: romance and danger. I agree with being cautious and wise; however, I'd been on staff long enough to know this wasn't the only reason the walls were sky high between the sexes. Our men had to learn to conduct off-line meetings in places other than their favorite cigar lounge (a place we women didn't frequent), and they had to adjust how they talked among themselves when we were present. I had to remind my husband, the pastor responsible for encouraging the staff, that we women didn't always want tickets to a baseball game or to a steak restaurant. Truth is: female presence changes things—and it's often uncomfortable for men to adjust to those changes. They have to give up some of their previous ways—ways they liked. Sex isn't the only thing in play, so is power.

---

31   While taking a course on sexuality and marriage at Regent College in Vancouver, a student stood and stated, "We can't talk about homosexuality because we haven't figured out how to talk about sexuality." I couldn't agree more.

I want us to be careful when dealing with the opposite sex, but not to the point where we miss the narrative of oneness within the community that Jesus and Paul both taught. Dan Brennan said it best:

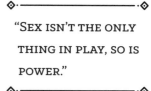

"SEX ISN'T THE ONLY THING IN PLAY, SO IS POWER."

The Gospel brings a new narrative, one that harks back to the Garden, Christ is reconciling sexuality and spirituality through his reign and his Spirit has given us all the resources we need to create a new community where men and women can live together without engaging in sexual immorality. Isn't this the story we find in the New Testament, a story where the fundamental attitudes towards one another is love that creates a non-romantic oneness among men and women? In Paul's letter to the Corinthians he addressed "brothers and sisters" over sixty times. His instructions on love found in 1 Corinthians 13 address attitudes not so much to individual relationship with God as the interaction between Christian brothers and sisters. The thirty-three "one anothers" are addressed to the community, brothers and sisters are to "care for one another" (1 Corinthians 12:25–26), "bear one another's burdens" (Galatians 5:22; 6:2), to "suffer and rejoice with one another" (Romans 12) and Colossians instructs Christian men and women to "put on, then, as God's chosen ones, holy and beloved, compassion, kindness, lowliness, meekness, and patience, forbearing each other... and above all these put on love, which binds everything together in perfect harmony" (Colossians 3;12–14).

In the New Testament the brother-sister metaphor "anticipates the embodied nearness between men and women for all eternity-and suggests we can experience some of that depth as we live between the already and not yet... In the new heavens and earth, Jesus said something significant will change in marriage (Matt. 22:30). Although we don't know what our future fully looks like it's evident we will live in eternity as brothers and sisters. It seems to me we should start learning now how to live like we will live in eternity.[32]

Brennan's views are not without controversy, and I'm not suggesting we embrace everything he teaches on the subject. But I do believe it's time we engage the Scripture with a new lens, a oneness lens. It's then we will find that God is in fact calling us beyond to something more radical than our romance-danger narrative. We talked about this openly on staff at IBC, and this openness enabled us to start to live like we will live in eternity: as brothers and sisters. That's when the walls will come tumbling down.

---

32   Dan Brennan, *Sacred Unions, Sacred Passions: Engaging the Mystery of Friendship Between Men and Women* (Faith Dance Publishing, 2010) p. 58.

Chapter Five

RIDING AND ROWING

My MIDDLE SON is Dennis the Menace on caffeine. And I'm putting that nicely! People used to tell me it was just his teenage hormones—hard to believe since he'd been this way since he was four. Back then, I did what all mothers do: I read all the books on parenting. Nothing worked. The last one I turned to was Dobson's *Bringing Up Boys,* which I threw against the wall and screamed, "What do you do when you've tried all that and nothing works?"

It was while lingering in some Old Testament passages that I learned parenting was like riding a wild horse. Listen to what the Prophet Ezekiel said: "I will give you a new heart, and I will put a new spirit in you. I will take out your stony, stubborn heart and give you a tender, responsive heart. And I will put my Spirit in you so that you will follow my decrees and be careful to obey my regulations" (Ezekiel 36:26–27).[33] Notice how many times God said, "I will." In this passage, God reminded me Hampton's heart was his to change—not mine. I realized I'd been going to all the wrong books. The Bible was the book on parenting I needed in that time. Because there Jesus would say, "Just stay on the horse."

---

33   Read a similar sentiment from God in Jeremiah 31:31–34.

I learned staying on the horse would look different in different situations. But it always meant turning to God's Word for direction. So, the day I received a phone call from the middle school vice principal informing me that Hampton had stolen an ice cream during lunch (how stupid considering he had $20 in his lunch account!), just as I had learned to do in that tiny apartment, I went to the Scriptures and asked Jesus, "Show me the issue. Tell me what to do." God led[34] me to Ephesians 4:28.[35]

When Hampton got home, I sat him down and said, "I received a call from your vice principal today." By the look on his face there was no need for further explanation.

"I asked Jesus what the heart issue was and here's what he wants to say to you: 'Hampton, quit stealing. Instead, use your hands for good hard work and give generously to others in need.' What that means is you are going to have to do some yard work for your dad. You'll get paid. And you'll give it to someone in need."

The beauty of Jesus parenting your child is it alleviates parental guilt. Whatever happens with your child is really between him and Jesus. Let that news sit on your child's shoulders! Just like the Scriptures said: Jesus knows my son's heart and what action will curtail the sin that lurks within as well as what action brings out the best in him.

For instance, Hampton has the spiritual gift of mercy. I've always said: if you're strong, you are Hampton's competitor, and he must take you down. But if you are hurt, Hampton is your warrior and will carry you to safety. God made him like that. That's why God instructed me to Ephesians 4:28. That verse hits the sin and the way to counter it.

---

34   Too often we are freaked by the idea of "God personally speaking to us." Scripture says that the Holy Spirit translates and explains to our hearts the Word (John 14:26 & 2 Timothy 3:16), so that we can appraise all things (1 Corinthians 2:15). As we struggle to know what God says about the circumstances in our lives, the Holy Spirit dispels the darkness by introducing the light (1 John 1:5) Trust God to speak!

35   "Anyone who has been stealing must steal no longer, but must work, doing something useful with their own hands, that they may have something to share with those in need." NIV

That day, Hampton worked in the yard with his dad, got paid, and then went to the corner of a highway where homeless men beg for money. He took his hard-earned money and bought a homeless man lunch. Now what do you think that does to a child's heart of mercy? Just as back in that tiny apartment I was learning how to go to Jesus first, now going to him was second nature.

"I have to ask Jesus about this and I'll get back to you" became my normal mom-response. I don't know if you've noticed, but Jesus can take a long time to answer! It drove my kids crazy. Days of waiting for a verdict and sentencing can be agonizing! And yet, when the verdict did come down, my kids knew their mother sought their Creator. He was personally instructing them. Another example of the beauty in the hard.

In April 2006, six weeks before the end of the school year, Hampton got thrown out of school.[36] His expulsion happened the same week I was to leave for my first year of residency at Gordon Conwell Theological Seminary. I was so looking forward to obtaining my preaching doctorate. It would not only help hone my preaching skills, but in the third year I would learn how to develop a homiletics (art of preaching) course. It was exactly what was needed to continue equipping women to teach the Scriptures effectively. But Hampton's circumstances left me burdened. *Where would he finish out his last month of school? How's this impacting him?* I decided I wouldn't go. My heart was such a mess I wouldn't be able to concentrate anyways. And besides, what kind of mother leaves home during a time like this? So I told my family I wasn't going.

And there was Steve, once again pushing me places I didn't want to go. With deep conviction, he said, "You are going! We are not letting this kid or anything else get in the way of what God has for your life. You're going!"

I've thought many times how desperately we need others to remind us of God's mark on our lives. We see this in 1 Samuel 23:17, where Jonathan went to find David and encouraged him to stay strong in his faith in God. "Don't

---

36   Lest some of you worry I'm "humiliating" my son by stating such things publicly, don't fret. He thinks he should get some kind of royalties for all the illustrations he's provided.

be afraid," Jonathan reassured David. "My father will never find you! You are going to be the king of Israel." Now I want you to think about this: technically, who in King Saul's family is next in line for the throne? Jonathan. Yet here's Jonathan, putting aside his own interests to encourage David. And how does he do that? *David, remember who you are! Think ahead to what God has for you to do!* Jonathan dreamed dreams for David—dreams that David could no longer dream for himself. I need that. You need that. Hampton needed that. We all need Jonathans and Steves in our lives. We women especially need them if we are to live out God's dreams for our lives.

———

The room was set up with four rectangle tables in a square formation. The professor was seated at the "front" of the class. As I stood in the doorway, I scanned the room for Maxie, the only other woman on the student roster. *Where is she? She must be late.* I hoped to sit next to her. Instead a middle-aged man waved for me to sit next to him. I was relieved he took the initiative. The rest of the class just stared, not knowing what to do with my presence. *When is Maxie coming?* Our professor went around the tables asking each of us to share something about ourselves. That's when I learned Maxie was a male pastor from Jamaica. Talk about disappointed. I would be the only female in a class of twenty-seven students, all male pastors and me.

Being a woman in a male-dominated field opened my eyes to the dire need of a different narrative. Without a different narrative, half the church is kept back from fully advancing the kingdom. The men in my class—and let me say they were wonderful, godly men—didn't have a clue what to do with me, a female embodied spirit.

For two weeks the guys headed out to lunch while I stayed behind eating alone in the lunchroom. I know they felt bad, but they had the romantic-danger narrative running through their heads. *You don't take a woman to lunch. You don't get in a car alone with a woman. You don't have a woman in your office with the door closed.* I felt cheated because I knew I was missing out on great off-line conversations about homiletics, church, the Kingdom, and such. I longed to benefit, grow, and be transformed; to have iron sharpen iron, but my body screamed *danger! danger!* to them, so I was left out.

The last day of our first-year residency, we were given an assignment: establish a cohort, a group of four to five classmates, to work with over the next several years. Suddenly the room felt like the kickball playground back in elementary. *Who's going to pick me? Will I be picked last? Who's going to take Jackie?* After some hesitation Bryan, Bill, Joel, and Mike picked me to be on their team. The only time available for us to discuss the upcoming project and schedule for achieving it was over lunch. Finally, I got to go to lunch with my classmates! The conversation was stimulating. The day Steve insisted "you're going," I had no idea that my doctorate would be exactly what I needed to bring joy in the midst of a storm at home.

That August we boarded an American Airlines flight to Richmond, Virginia. We had decided Hampton would spend his ninth-grade year at Fork Union Military Academy. We arrived two weeks early so that Hampton could try out for soccer. Several hours after landing we ended up at a "doc in the box" only to discover Hampton had pneumonia.

That night as Steve and Hampton lay asleep, I called my mom and just sobbed. I couldn't speak coherently. Mom just listened. After I hung up the phone, I continued sobbing to Jesus. *What should we do? Do I stay and make sure he gets healthy before going back to Texas?* Jesus simply said, *Trust me. Let me parent him, Jackie. Go home.*

The following day, pneumonia and all, we dropped him off at his new school. As we drove away, I looked back and there he was, barely 5-feet-tall and 115-pounds, wearing gray military shorts and t-shirt standing next to a huge dude there for football tryouts. Leaving him behind felt like someone had taken a baseball bat to my stomach. I bawled, snot dripping out, all the way to the airport.

The next morning I went to the gym, thinking exercise would help my state of being. A woman from church came up and asked how I was doing.

"Horrible!" I told her, then proceeded to share how we had just dropped off Hampton in Virginia.

"I'm surprised you're taking it so hard," she said. "I mean, you're so spiritual and all."

I've never gotten used to people's perceptions of ministers—as if we aren't human. I quickly reminded the woman, "If you cut me, I'd bleed just like you."

Cadets weren't allowed to contact their parents for six weeks after drop off. For six weeks, I worried about his pneumonia and how he was faring in his two-a-day soccer tryouts. I had grown up learning to do hard, but having my son gone was one of the hardest things I've ever done. Thoughts like, *what if he's raped at that all-boy school?* agonized me. Many times I was overcome with deep sadness—especially nights when I looked into his empty bedroom. Once again I found myself on the proverbial couch, wrestling with God about my kids. "God, you know kids don't fare well when they've been raped. Or bullied. Or..." Once again the sweet whispers[37] of my Savior gave assurance, not that Hampton would be safe, but that, no matter what, he had him. Jesus would parent him when I could not. Over and over I would have to trust and entrust my kids to God, and to keep turning to the Scriptures for the wisdom I needed as a woman navigating some new territory.

Housing for my second-year residency was a continued reminder that my female body was "a problem." As the only woman, I was housed in a separate place from the men. I stayed in a big old musty-smelling inn with dark hallways, just outside of the Boston city limits—alone, all by myself. The

---

37   It was a woman preacher God used to whisper assurance. Anne Graham Lotz preached on Isaiah 6:1, "I saw the Lord sitting on a lofty throne, and the train of his robe filled the Temple." That verse was the whisper my heart needed to hear. My life was in chaos but God's was not. He was still on his throne, in charge, in control. My chaos was not chaos for him.

male students stayed together in the yellow house adjacent to the inn. To attend class, we drove fifteen minutes to an area of Boston deemed not "all that safe." At least, that was the warning given by the seminary. A warning that turned out to be warranted since a man was murdered outside our building during our residency.

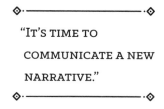

The night I arrived at the inn, I made up my mind to catch a ride with one of the guys, at least for the first day or until I felt secure driving by myself. The next morning I walked into the breakfast area where all the guys were eating. I noticed Bill, one of my cohorts, sitting a few tables back to my right. My built-up fear of feeling unsafe at the seminary burst while I stood at the entrance of the room. "Bill," I blurted out, for all to hear, "can you give me a ride to class?"

Everyone froze, mid-motion, spoons and coffee cups suspended in mid-air. I stood there thinking, *oh brother, you've got to be kidding me?* Once again I faced down that romantic-danger narrative. Their fear of me, my womanhood, overshadowed my legitimate fear for my safety. Good Christian men would rather "protect" themselves (fear of lust) than protect a neighbor. I had had it. I wasn't going to let it dominate the landscape anymore. I wanted more for me—and them. So I did what I learned to do growing up: I called it out. Isn't that what we teach? That communication is key to relationships? I decided it was time to communicate a new narrative. I hoped my narrative would put them at ease, and we could get to learning homiletics together. So, standing there, overlooking the room I said, "I don't want to have sex with you. I just want a ride. As your sister in Christ, I want a ride because I'm afraid. I don't want to get raped." There was this nervous chuckle, but also an awkward relief because we had gotten it out in the open. We finished eating breakfast, and I caught a ride to class with Bill.

Now I know what some are thinking: *But Jackie, aren't we "playing with fire" by insisting on a different narrative?* No, in fact I think brother-sister narrative is a biblical narrative that has gotten lost and is long overdue in our oversexed culture. Contemporary Christian thinkers like Scot McKnight, N.T. Wright, and Jonalyn Fincher are beginning a new conversation about how our future relationships in the new heavens and new earth might look in the here-and-now.

Theologians and ministers alike are asking questions from passages in Scripture like John 17: 11, 20–23,[38] where Jesus prays for "oneness" (the same word that's used in Genesis 2:24) of the community, brothers, and sisters. (Something Paul spoke of way more than he spoke of marriage.) They are taking into account that the brother-sister relationship is the one that carried into the new heavens and new earth. The brother-sisterhood narrative forces us to reckon that the garden story is about more than marriage: It's about man and woman in community, male and female acting as a royal priesthood, ruling and subduing the whole earth on God's behalf—*together.*

Walk with me for a minute in the garden with this oneness of community in mind. Though most of us have been taught to think about the passage solely in terms of marriage, let's try, just for a minute. In Genesis 2:18, God said it is *"not good for man to be alone. I will make a helper suitable* [ezer kenego] *for him."*

What should we expect God to do next? *Create woman, right?* We can't be known if we aren't in community, right? So it seems logical God should create woman. But he doesn't.

Instead there's this long pause, some speculate over a hundred years, where God sends Man to name the animals. Now why does God do that? How does naming the animals solve the "aloneness" problem? Let's take a stroll with Man and listen in. He sees a frog. *I'll call you frog. But I'm not a frog.*

---

38   Jesus prayed, "Holy Father protect them … so that they may be one as we are one." (v. 11) "that all of them may be one, Father, just as you are in me and I am in you" (v. 21). Christ desired that his church would be the earthly community of oneness modeled after the eternal community of oneness. Gilbert Bilezikian, *Community 101* (Grand Rapids, Mich.: Zondervan, 2009) pp. 35–37.

Dog. I'll call you dog. But I'm not a dog. Pig. I'll call you pig. But I'm not a pig.

What's happening? As he names the animals, Man discovers who he is *not*. He's not a frog or a dog. His aloneness is exacerbated. Then God put Man to sleep and brought him *ezer kenego*. Listen to what Man said: "At last! This one is bone from my bone and flesh from my flesh! She will be called 'woman'…" (Genesis 2:23). This is not just some "Hey, check out my hot wife!" as some pastors claim. The expression is one of wonder. When God brought Woman to Man, he recognized Woman was more like him than any other creature. And her sameness enabled him to know himself. But her difference (*ezer kenego* can mean face to face opposition) moves him out of self and into otherness, a.k.a., community. It's through Woman that Man discovers his true self-nature—to be relational. There's an African word, *ubuntu,* which sums it up. It means: "A person is a person through [other] persons."[39]

Now it makes sense that God would want Man to know this about himself (and Woman about herself). He's placed them both on earth to act as his regency: authority on earth. And they must do it in community because that's who God is: three in one. Have you ever stepped back and realized that God, by his very nature, exists in relationship? He is never apart from relationship. It's who he is. God, by nature, exists in relationship; wouldn't it make sense that we, who were made in his image, were made to be in relationship too? Of course, this can mean in marriage, but as suggested above, it also represents the community of oneness.

With this in mind now, try to hear anew God's words in Genesis 1:26–28:

Then God said, "Let **us** make mankind in **our** image, in **our** likeness, so that they may **rule** over the fish in the sea and the birds in the sky, over the livestock and all the wild animals, and over all the

---

39   Scot McKnight, Scot, *One Life* (Grand Rapids, Mich. Zondervan, 2010) p. 32.

creatures that move along the ground."

So God created mankind in his own image, in the image of God he created them; male and female he created them.

God blessed them and said to them, "Be fruitful and increase in number; *fill the earth [this is not unique to humans[40]]* and *subdue it. Rule [this is unique to humans]* over the fish in the sea and the birds in the sky and over every living creature that moves on the ground." (Italics mine).

Male and female—humans—are made in the image and likeness of God, with a royal-priestly mission to flourish and fill the earth. Scot McKnight explains like this: "The creation of the world as God's temple, the placing of two little Eikons – Adam and Eve as divine image-bearers—in the garden temple of God (called Eden) to represent God; to govern for God; and to relate to God, self, others, and the world in a redemptive way."[41]

Carolyn Custis James echoes:

God designed the world to stand on two load-bearing walls. The first load-bearing wall is God's relationship with his image bearers. Without this vital relationship, we are cut off from our life supply—homeless, stranded souls in the universe, left to guess at who we are and why we

---

40   And God said, "Let the water teem with living creatures, and let birds fly above the earth across the vault of the sky." So God created the great creatures of the sea and every living thing with which the water teems and that moves about in it, according to their kinds, and every winged bird according to its kind. And God saw that it was good. God blessed them and said, "Be fruitful and increase in number and fill the water in the seas, and let the birds increase on the earth." Genesis 1:20–22

41   McKnight goes on to say, "The single task of representing God and governing God's garden was radically distorted when Adam and Even rebelled against the good command of God...Notice this: what God does in sending the Son is to establish Jesus as the Messiah, which means King, and God established in Jesus Christ the kingdom of God, which means the King is ruling in his kingdom. We need to restate this: the idea of King and a kingdom are connected to the original creation. God wanted the Eikons, Adam and Eve, to rule this world. They failed, so God sent his son to rule." Scot McKnight, *The King Jesus Gospel* (Grand Rapids, Mich.: Zondervan, 2011) pp. 35–36.

are here. The second load-bearing wall is the Blessed Alliance between male and female. According to Genesis, male/female relationships aren't simply necessary to perpetuate the human race and make life pleasurable and interesting.

Male/female relationships are strategic. God laid out his game plan in Genesis, and the team he assembled to do the job was male and female. Men and women working together actually predates men working with men and women working with women. It would be one thing if God confined this male/female team to home and family and then mapped out the remaining territory into separate spheres for men and for women. But he didn't do that. Their mission—together—is to rule and subdue the whole earth on his behalf. Men and women together. Our relationships with God and with each other are the load-bearing walls of God's original design.[42]

The point I'm trying to make is we are in need of a new narrative, one that harkens back to the old one, the narrative that more accurately depicts God's

> "A ROMANTIC-DANGER NARRATIVE SPLINTERS AND DIVIDES, AND PERHAPS MORE IMPORTANTLY, MISREPRESENTS GOD'S ONENESS."

original plan and purpose for male and female. A romantic-danger narrative splinters and divides, and perhaps more importantly, misrepresents God's oneness.

"When men are called to full-fledged kingdom living but the other half of the church is asked to sit on the sidelines, there is no Blessed Alliance, the bride of Christ limps, and we misrepresent God's oneness."[43] We need a story that points people to God's image when they see us, men and women, as

---

42   Custis Carolyn James, *Half The Church* (Grand Rapids, Mich.: Zondervan, 2010) p. 40.

43   Custis Carolyn James, *Half The Church* (Grand Rapids, Mich.: Zondervan, 2010) p. 140.

individuals and together. We need a story where we rediscover our need for one another to bring out the best in each other, to equip us all for Kingdom work. Because let's be real: people are living in hell and heading straight there for eternity. We can't afford to have people standing on the sidelines. We need a story where God's people, male and female, are advancing the Kingdom in full strength. Will it be messy? Absolutely. We don't live in utopia; the church exists in all its rugged messiness, struggling towards its glorious future. That's what I was fighting for that morning at breakfast—a different biblical narrative. Graciously, my brothers accepted the challenge.

—

On Monday April 16, 2007, news broke of a Virginia Tech student who shot and killed thirty-two other students. Although our country had suffered previous school shootings, this one is etched into my mind. I was in my musty-smelling room preparing a first-person message for the next day's class when my sister called. Her voice cracked. I knew immediately it was about my dad. My parents had recently separated due to my dad's erratic behavior. He had started doing dangerous things with dangerous people and by doing so, endangered my extended family. So at age sixty, after forty years of marriage, my mother asked Dad to move out. She remained in the main home while he went to live in their smaller home on the farm property.

When they separated, we kids were left with the task of helping mom unravel their forty years of life together. Dad wasn't real pleased when we had him removed as president, or when we restricted his access to the finances, or when we insisted on the closing of two of his businesses. It was painful to watch my mom deal with the shock and grief, to see my dad going off the wall, and to watch my younger siblings try to navigate business in the middle of it all. Over the past year, I had received many calls dealing with my parents' situation. That's how I knew this one was one of "those calls."

What I didn't know is this time things had escalated to a place we all had hoped it wouldn't. My sister unfolded the story of late: My dad had walked into his office and announced he "could do something like that guy at Virginia Tech."

My family was shaken and in disbelief. Who really believes these things will happen to them? A few hours later a relative called to warn my sister because Dad said he'd been having "visions" of killing her. And that those visions had become clearer and more defined. My family feared my dad was about to do something horrible. Given that dad kept guns in his house, my terrified family contacted the police. My dad spent the night in jail.

I hung up the phone and felt numb. Overwhelmed. Unsteady. Alone. Afraid. *Should I go to my mom's? Should Steve come and help? How do I get through this night?* All night my head spun, my heart cracked, fear twirled, and my body ached. In the morning I got my period. Though it freaks people out when I mention this (but come on, you know women my age get their period, right?), it played a part in my state of being. And yet, despite my unsteady state, I went to class to preach my first ever first-person message without notes. I have no idea how I got through it. That morning I lived what Paul said in Philippians 4:13, "I can do everything through Christ who gives me strength." It was like an out-of-body experience, but somehow I nailed it. Well, I nailed it with two exceptions: Dr. Haddon Robinson suggested I learn to control the higher pitches in my voice,[44] and one student was concerned about my personal sharing.

Previously in class, Haddon leaned over and asked, "Jackie, do you think women see the text differently than men?" At first I protested. Was he implying men contemplate the higher things whereas women think of "lower things"? But that's not what he was saying at all. In fact, Haddon was challenging me to research the differences so I could come to understand and use my female voice to preach God's Word. What I discovered is women see and speak Scripture differently (whether that's due to DNA or social development is up for debate). The differences are laid out in detail in my previous

---

44   Women use approximately five tones whereas men use only three. This is important because those emotionally laden words with tone range can make a woman sound more emotional than a man. Not that she is emotional but she *sounds* emotional. Perhaps a reason some men struggle listening to female teachers, particularly those who have full range of tones.

63

book.[45] In essence: women tend to see the Scriptures from a relational, inter-dependent, communal lens, whereas men tend to see the text from an inde-pendent, analytical (usually hierarchical) mindset. This impacts how one speaks of Scripture. Women tend to speak of the relationships, are more vulnerable, and use more personal story than men. This is why my personal story unnerved the male student. Haddon told the student who complained that the pulpit would benefit from more personal authenticity. (I love that man. Did I mention that? As a brother, of course.)

After class I dragged my achy mind, body, and soul back to my room.

I got another call.

My sister and mom had just returned from the courthouse. That morn-ing, my dad— wearing an orange jumpsuit and handcuffs—was shuffled in front of a judge. The judge ordered my dad to be evaluated at a psych hospi-tal. He was released a few days later. We never found out the results.

Our family continued down this unknown road of unraveling.

—

My last residency, in the spring of 2008, was much better than the pre-vious. Hampton was back home and doing well in his new school. For now things were calm with my extended family. And this year, instead of being at the old inn, I was housed in a hotel along with all the other students. Slowly the guys and I were becoming more of a community of oneness. All was mov-ing along well. Then Steve called. Hampton was put on probation because he used profanity in class. (It wasn't even a really bad swear word either! Ugh.) Now Steve and I had to decide to pull him now or wait to see if he could make it through the year. If he committed another infraction, he would have to leave and we would lose the paid tuition. Once again my heart broke, and once again Steve had to handle the situation back home while I was away. Back on my knees I went. *What now Jesus? Show us what to do!*

Sometimes God speaks to me through picture—images. They stick. A while back he had given me a picture of Hampton: A wild bunking bronco.

---

45   In chapter 4 of my book, *She Can Teach: Empowering Women to Teach the Scrip-tures Effectively*, I address the female voice in preaching.

I was riding; not well, mind you. There were times I was riding sideways, or my head was banging on the ground while riding upside down. My hair was flying every which way, pants ripped, and dirt covered my skin. This was the picture God gave.

His instructions, "Just stay on."

"No matter what, stay on."

The sight brought out the barging mother within, "If I stay on, will you bring him through?" I wanted a guarantee: If I were faithful, would God promise Hampton's life would go well?

What I got instead was: *What if he doesn't straighten up and his life is a mess all the way to the end?* God wasn't giving a guarantee. In fact, I sensed he wasn't all that concerned about the outcome as much as my faithfulness. Would I be faithful no matter what? That's what he was concerned with.

When you have a wayward child, that's hard to hear. A mother wants assurance.

I remember being led to meditate on 1 Peter 1:6–7

So be truly glad. There is wonderful joy ahead, even though you have to endure many trials for a little while. These trials will show that your faith is genuine. It is being tested as fire tests and purifies gold—though your faith is far more precious than mere gold. So when your faith remains strong through many trials, it will bring you much praise and glory and honor on the day when Jesus Christ is revealed to the whole world.

Do you get what he's saying? Faithfulness is more precious than gold. Faith—my faith, your faith—is precious to Jesus. The passage seems to be saying that Jesus is going to *praise* us for our faith. Imagine, being praised by God himself! Almost sounds sacrilegious, doesn't it? But it's there in the Scriptures.

Jesus gave me a picture—that wild horse—then said, "Just stay on." Regardless of whether or not Hampton was at this school or that school, doing this or that, I was not giving up. I was determined to love him unconditionally. My mom loved me like that and her fleshly example enabled me to receive Christ's unconditional, unlimited love. Now, Jesus was asking for me to love like I had been loved. We moved Hampton from Christian school to public school—and I was still on the horse.

—

A woman once commented how hard my doctorate must be in light of working full-time and raising three teenage kids. I chuckled. She wasn't aware that my parents were imploding and my husband had been diagnosed with a benign brain tumor and that I walked around with continuous back pain. The two cracked bones became arthritic, and I had degenerative disease in three discs. My doctor said my back looked like a football player's. (Turned out all that bending and lifting in the fields during the years of puberty did lots of damage.) And this woman thought my doctorate was hard! Little did she know my doctorate was a minor detail. In fact, it was a delight in the midst of the other storms raging around me.

But again God was good. He gave another picture, one that would teach me how to endure. First Corinthians 4:1–2 says, "Let a man regard us in this manner, as servants of Christ and stewards of the mysteries of God" (NAS). A steward is a servant who's been given responsibility for the master's home. A bit of a cushy job really, especially when compared to the other servants. The root meaning behind *servant* is an under-rower. Think of Charlton Heston in the movie *Ben-Hur*. He's been enslaved, put in the bowels of a ship, ankles chained to the floor while he sits on a hard, wooden bench, two oars in his hands, and like all the other slaves around him, he rows. The captain of the ship is above deciding direction and dictating instructions. The under-rower's job is to row. They row when they want to and when they don't. They row when they're rested and when they're tired. They just row.

I needed that picture. I stowed the image in my mind as I rowed through those years. Sometimes it's where we find ourselves isn't it? In the bowels of life with no control, so we just row. That's where I was. So I rowed. I rowed when I wanted to and when I didn't want to. I rowed when I wanted to give up and when I was tired. I just rowed. I didn't always like rowing—many times I cussed, worse than Hampton. Sometimes I had to see a counselor because I was crashing, but I rowed none-the-less. Sometimes all we can do is row, but we row with assurance because our Captain is Jesus. He's on the deck directing, and he has our best in mind.

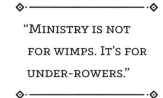

"MINISTRY IS NOT FOR WIMPS. IT'S FOR UNDER-ROWERS."

—

On one of the last days of class Troy, a young, handsome inner-city preacher gave me some of the best advice I'd ever received. "Jackie," he said, "I hope you don't take this the wrong way, but you're not humble."

Hmmm. Just which "right" way was I supposed to take this? Handling constructive criticism is hard, but the Bible says if we listen to constructive criticism, we will be "at home among the wise" (Proverb15: 31).

I swallowed my pride and gathered my surprise. "What makes you say that?" I asked.

He continued, "I've watched you in class and you feel the need to justify your being here. I want to give you a definition of humility. Breathe it in Jackie and live it out."

He quoted author James Riley in his definition of *humility*. Humility is, he said, "the God-given self-assurance that eliminates the need to prove to others the worth of who you are and the rightness of what you do."

And there it was—a brother fighting for me. His words gave new life to my soul. I hadn't realized it. It wasn't intentional. But there was fear, the fear of being hammered by those who oppose a woman preaching. So I had put on boxing gloves, raised my arms high and waited for the first punch to fly. Troy was right. I felt the need to justify my being there, to prove I was right in what I did, that is, preach. When he said those words, I had no idea that in just four short months, I would want to put those gloves back on. I had no idea my calling to preach was about to be publically challenged.

During my doctoral years I learned ministry is not for wimps. It's for under-rowers. Men and women sitting side-by-side rowing when they want to and when they don't, rowing together because they trust where their Captain Jesus is taking them.

Chapter Six

CHANGE HAPPENS
SLOWLY

O UR FAMILY SPENT summers going to Gilbert Lake, a small lake about fifteen minutes from our house. Though there were several lifeguard stations, only one had a certain whistle. *That* whistle was blown to alert everyone that someone had gone under the water and not come back up. When we heard that whistle, everyone present lined up along the shore, linked arms and started dredging the lake. The hope was that one of us would bump into the person who had gone under in time to save his or her life.

Can you imagine the person under water looking at the line and saying something like, "Man, I can't have that *black* guy save me!" or "I can't have a *woman* save me!"?

Absurd, right? And can you imagine if someone on the shore refused to link arms with people because they weren't the right age, color, shape, religious belief, or gender? Again, absurd. Because then there'd be a gap in the link, and that gap may very well be where the person lay under water—dying. I picture a guy under water screaming, "Hurry! Link up! Someone, anyone, find me!"

Figuratively speaking, a whole lot of people have sunk under the water, dying little deaths and big deaths all over the place. Did you know there are 160 million street children and 300 million child laborers? Did you know the sex industry is a 97.06 billion dollar worldwide business and that there are more strip clubs in the United States than any other nation? Did you know seven young people from the class of 2007 in my suburban city have either committed suicide, overdosed or been killed in a car accident? Did you know some of my relatives are drowning under water? Some of yours are too. There are people outside and inside our churches drowning. Those people can't afford for us Christians to stand on the shore fighting or dredging the lake with gaps in the line because we're too busy arguing over who gets to do what. As Dorothy Sayers wrote, when it comes to doing life- and soul-saving work in the kingdom of God: "As we cannot afford to squander our natural resources of minerals, food, and beauty, so we cannot afford to discard any human resources of brains, skills, and initiative even though it is women who possess them."[46]

And yet, as I followed my calling to teach the Word of God to those who desperately needed to hear it—to be saved by it—I realized just how many of my fellow believers didn't mind these "gaps in the line" of Kingdom work and who were willing to let people "drown" rather than hear the Gospel from the wrong kind of preacher. A preacher like me.

Because of passages like Paul's words to Timothy,[47] throughout church history there has been much confusion about the roles of women in the church. It's messy to discern how, when or where a woman can join the line. The lines are blurred within church and from church to church. Because Paul wrote, "I do not permit a woman to teach or have authority over a man,"[48] churches ask questions like:

"Can a woman teach middle school boys?"

"Can she collect the tithe on Sunday?"

---

46   Dorothy Sayers, *Are Women Human* (Grand Rapids, Mich.: Eerdmans, 2003).

47   1 Timothy 2–3

48   1 Timothy 2:12

"Can a man listen to a female teacher's podcast?"

"What about reading a woman's book?"[49]

It's not clear. In fact it's so unclear that the Council on Biblical Manhood and Womanhood (CBMW) has written an extensive list[50] of what women should and shouldn't do in the church. The reality is the complementarian view forces churches to convolute themselves into all sorts of contortions to make everything fit. Just listen to this woman's story of how her church played the "Twister" game.

> My husband and I both graduated from seminary. He was on the pastoral staff of a large church in Texas. I too serve in ministry but in a more unconventional way.
>
> Our church came to me and asked if I would write curriculum for one of their adult Sunday school classes. Once the writing was finished a team of us would teach the material. I was excited at the opportunity. My husband is a good teacher, but he would not be part of our team because of his other pastoral responsibilities on Sundays. I was good with that.
>
> After writing was finished I met with one of the pastors to find out what was next. He informed me I needed to find a man to be on the team as the leader.
>
> He continued, "This man doesn't have to teach. He can sit in the back and listen. But he needs to be there for headship purposes."
>
> I laughed. Surely he was kidding? He wasn't.

---

49   In *The Blue Parakeet,* McKnight makes the argument: "Anyone who thinks its wrong for a woman to teach in a church can be consistent with that point of view only if they refuse to read and learn from women scholars. This means not reading their books lest they become teachers" (p. 148).

50   cbmw.org/wp-content/uploads/2013/05/1–2.pdf Their list contains 28 suggestions for the "Area of Governing Authority," 35 suggestions for Bible teaching, and 20 suggestions for areas of visibility or recognition.

I joked, "Would any man do?"

He responded, "Well, yes. Any man would do."

My friend confided that she wondered if the homeless guy on the corner would suffice, so long as there was a man sitting in the back of the room. She declined the offer because, in her opinion, their line seemed "nonsensical."

It was true of my friend's church, and it was true of ours too. Consider what our senior pastor Andy McQuitty said:

> Almost every year we'd have something erupt, something we'd have to try to patch up and figure out. Okay, how do we handle this? In our church we had crazy things like how old does a young man need to be in order for a woman to be disqualified from teaching him? In our youth ministry, we've had female leaders working with the kids. A woman can teach children, including boys, but when does a boy become a man? Is it like the Jewish bar mitzvah? All of the sudden, we can't have our female counselors doing any Bible teaching because they'd be teaching men. Another inconsistency was, in our adult Sunday school classes we usually had adult teachers but sometimes couples would team-teach. We were in a dilemma because some days, a woman is doing pretty much all of the teaching with men present, so how do we get around that? We'd say 'I suppose a woman can't preach from the pulpit.' But can she go into the pulpit and read Scripture and comment on its basic meaning? We actually had that happen at one point. "Sue Edwards went up and read some Scripture and made a few comments. And we heard from people, who asked, 'Was she preaching?' And no she wasn't preaching, but it was a very simple thing that she was doing, and when we heard the uproar from that, it just struck as really odd.

Inconsistencies in praxis had existed at Irving Bible Church, my home church, since its inception, but much like what we saw in Galileo's day, our time demands a fresh look at the Scriptures.

"INCARNATION CHANGES THINGS."

Some cry foul to this, saying Feminism is what's driving this, not the Holy Spirit. I don't deny that the Women's Rights movement has impacted part of our time in history. Feminism has left its mark not only on culture, but also on and in the church. However, I don't find the impact all bad—as some imply. For instance, surely most conservative faith communities would say it's a good thing women can vote, own property, and earn an equal wage for equal work. Regardless of where you stand on Women's Rights, in the church it merely cracked the doors open. What *flung* them open were incarnate relationships. I remember Dr. Sarah Sumner telling me as much years ago—that knowing and trusting a woman gifted with preaching, teaching, or leadership could change a "biblical" perspective. At first, I didn't want to believe her. But I came to learn she was right.

Incarnational relationships[51]—truly knowing and understanding one another in community—change things. Have you ever noticed how much easier it is to be mean spirited behind someone's back than to their face? Incarnation changes things. It's true with our theology also. It's much easier to make theological propositions about women's issues or homosexuality, for instance, until they affect our daughters, our sons, our close friends. Incarnation changes things. We learned this when the Word became Flesh, when Jesus himself was God incarnate here on earth. Isn't that how we know God, through his embodied life? Jesus taught in human flesh because incarnation changes things.

"So the Word became human and made his home among us...He revealed God to us" (John 1:14, 18).

---

51   One of the best books I've read on this subject is Michael Frost's *Incarnate: The Body of Christ in an Age of Disengagement.*

Listen to how incarnational relationships started to impact Pastor Andy:

We wanted our gifted women to be able to express themselves and do everything that God equipped them to do. But we had to feather them in around the edges and finesse the tradition and theology that would keep them from doing anything. With Jackie on staff, with the thriving women's ministry that she and Sue Edwards and Julie Pierce were running at IBC, all of that came to a head. We had a real wealth of gifted, sharp ladies who could teach and lead. They were everywhere. I'd come walking in and I'd think, *You know what? We've got to do something to let these ones gifted by God do everything God has called them to do.*

Can you hear it? Pastor Andy started to see gaps in the line—some arms were not linked and people were drowning in the lake. This no longer made sense to him. He had pastored for years with one understanding but now, with the additional benefit of incarnational relationships, he questioned his understanding. And Pastor Andy saw it as an opportunity to revisit the Scriptures and what the Holy Spirit might be calling our church toward.

I sensed Pastor Andy, and others like him, walked away from seminary much like I did—as received knowers. Their stance on women was settled in a classroom way back when and now the hectic life of the pastorate made researching it again—at least in a serious manor—too difficult. It demanded too much time and energy. We all know it's easier to stick with what we learned a long time ago in a class.

That is, until the Holy Spirit beckons and we can ignore it no longer. Until there is relationship that calls us back to the text—to see with new eyes, through incarnational lenses.

While our senior pastor was feeling uneasy about the limitations of gifted women, still other male pastors were disconcerted by how female pastors where treated for doing "their job." For instance, Shelly, our youth pastor, was approached by a man after a Wednesday night middle school gathering to be informed she had sinned for "teaching boys." She was upset by the confusion.

Her job was okay with the pastoral staff, but apparently not okay with a man in the congregation. Which was right? As one male pastor stated, "While we had a culture of women in leadership, we also had a culture of not answering these questions. So people would sometimes turn a corner and face things they had not anticipated. It would either hurt them deeply or cause them to question, 'Have I just sinned?' And so we began to have this discussion. At least at the staff level. But it hit a wall at the elder level—at least at first blush."

At first the elders didn't see a need for the discussion. After all, comparatively, our church was very open to women serving in a variety of ways. Although that was true, it was also true—whether our elders realized it or not (and most did not)—that they were blinded by their privileged position.

Many people in power positions miss what's happening to those who aren't. In her book, *Lean In*, Sheryl Sandberg writes, "Men at the top are often unaware of the benefits they enjoy simply because they're men, and this can make them blind to the disadvantages associated with being a woman."[52]

Our elders were upper middle class, white males with "traditional" (meaning husband is the breadwinner and wife is the stay-at-home mom) marriages. Their positions within culture, the church and marriage blinded them to their privilege.

Sandberg also cites a 2012 series of studies that "compared men in more 'modern' marriages (whose wives worked outside the home full-time) to men in more 'traditional' marriages (whose wives were homemakers). The researchers wanted to determine if a man's home arrangement affected his professional behavior. It did. Compared to men in modern marriages, men in more traditional marriages viewed the presence of women in the workforce less favorable. They also denied promotions to qualified female employees more often and were more likely to think that companies with a higher percentage of female employees ran less smoothly. The researchers speculated that men in traditional marriages are not overtly hostile toward woman but instead are 'benevolent sexists'—holding positive yet outdated views about

---

52   Sheryl Sandberg, *Lean In* (New York: Knopf, 2013) p. 150.

women. These men might even believe that women have superior strengths in certain areas like moral reasoning, which makes them better equipped to raise children—yet perhaps less equipped to succeed in business. In all likelihood, men who share this attitude are unaware how their conscious and unconscious beliefs hurt their female colleagues."[53]

Our evangelical churches are full of male leaders who are *unaware* how their female colleagues experience ministry life. They are *blinded*.

Of course, we're all blinded in one-way or the other. In *Pursuing Justice*, Ken Wytsma reminds us that our "race, gender, class and education have shaped us to recognize some facets of justice and injustice more readily—and to be blind to issues that are clear to our brothers and sisters who are different from us."[54] This was true of our elders, and it is true of me too.

One Tuesday morning my colleague Julie Pierce and I invited Ana, (who worked in a secular job full time, attended seminary, and volunteered countless hours investing in the Spanish-speaking women in our church) to share how we could undergird her and the Spanish-speaking women better. In our ignorance, we thought we had done such a great job. How wrong we were! As Ana answered our question, I wanted to slump down under the table in embarrassment. For years us teachers transcribed our messages, which Ana translated and then made copies for each woman to read as the teacher preached from the front. Sheepishly she said, "Simultaneous translation would help."

Duh!

And if we wanted the Spanish-speaking women to attend the women's retreat we might want to advertise it in Spanish, she suggested.

Oh, yeah! That!

And a sign in Spanish pointing new women to the Bible study room would help.

Indeed.

---

53   Sandberg, p. 153.

54   Ken Wytsma, *Pursuing Justice* (Nashville: Thomas Nelson, 2013) p. 13.

She went on and on, and I, metaphorically speaking, slid under the table. My own major blind-spot toward the Spanish-speaking women of our church reminded me of the grace I needed to show our elders and their blind-spots. I needed to remove my blinders, as much as the elders needed to remove theirs.

So what was the first step towards removing the blinders in our church? You guessed it! By being incarnational. This began to take shape during one meeting when the elders looked around the room and realized these seven guys were discussing an issue about women without women. They decided it would be valuable to hear from women as to their experience of being a woman in ministry. So, on November 27, 2006, the elders invited several women from different ages, stages and churches from around the Dallas Fort Worth area to a "dine and dialogue." As we gathered together, they shared how the evening wasn't an evening of debate. They had invited us to "hear from us about our real life experiences in the church" (local *and* global church).

As this was announced, you could "hear" the disbelief within the women in the room.

They want to hear what we've experienced?

The elders sat quietly waiting and we women sat quietly nervous.

Slowly some women started to share.

A woman shared how her dad raised her to believe she was bright, capable, and could do anything. But then she went to seminary where she ran into roadblocks. Another young woman told of working hard in seminary and having a male student tell her, "I don't know why you are working so hard. You really just need to get married and have babies anyway." Another shared how she'd spent so much time and energy preparing a lesson only to be questioned by others in the congregation because young boys were in the audience. Another women confessed her shock going from the business world to the church world. Women shared how they had no voice, no decision-making power. They told of the times their work was invisible or taken for granted—especially as most worked for no pay. There were stories of feeling devalued, invisible, marginalized, and silenced.

Our elders hadn't expected any of it. They were shocked. By the end of the evening, many were in tears as they thought of their own daughters. The idea of *their* girls receiving these kinds of messages, this treatment, was not acceptable. It was a somber night of storytelling.

We see something similar happening back at the Jerusalem Council in Acts 15. Back in the First-Century Church, the brewing controversy wasn't the "women issue," it was the denial of salvation for Gentile believers who had not been circumcised (meaning, they had not kept the Jewish Law). Just like today, there were opposing camps vehemently arguing for their position as being the "biblical" one. The Jewish hardliners took the "biblical" approach against Barnabas and Paul's more "liberal" policy towards the Gentiles. In my opinion, the Jewish "hard liners" possessed the most ammunition. They had history on their side. Traditionally, the Torah had been interpreted to mandate categorically—without negotiation—circumcision. It was right there in the text! It was "clear." Ever heard that word used in reference to the women's debate? First Timothy 2 is "clear": women can't lead or teach men. That's what the Jewish hardliners could have said too. "It's clear."

Interestingly, the preponderance of ammunition was also on the side of those who supported slavery in America. There are plenty of Scriptures (Genesis 9:25–27, Ephesians 6:5–9, Colossians 3:22, Colossians 4:1, Titus 2:9, 1 Peter 2:18 just to list a few) to support their position, and tradition was certainly on their side.

One of the ways the First-Century Church resolved the conflict was by inviting members to share their stories—much like the elders did at our dine and dialogue. The passage reveals the numerous voices at the table—so to speak—during the deliberations. We have the Apostles and elders, the whole body of members, brothers, men, certain ones, key individuals (Paul and Barnabas), and the prophets (Judas and Silas Acts 15:32). It was at the table Barnabas and Paul told "the story about the miraculous signs and wonders God had done among the Gentiles through them" (15:12). Peter and James also reminded the people about Peter's episode with Cornelius (10:44–46).

The point is they heard from differing views and voices to find common ground. Healthy conflict resolution incorporates shared experiences from diverse voices. But how many of our churches make decisions about the roles of women without the voices of women? That's a problem. It's unwise. In light of Acts 15, it's even unbiblical. What might we be missing by such exclusion?

But there are more than just shared stories and multiple voices. We don't decide our theology based on experience alone. No, we go back to the Scriptures to see if they agree with what's being said. That's what the Berean Church did in Acts 17, and it's what James did at the Jerusalem Council. And it's what the elders of IBC did in 2008. James concluded that the words of the prophets Amos and Isaiah were in agreement with Paul and Barnabas' teaching (Acts 15:16–18). Our elders did the same. They went back to the Scriptures. They approached God's Word with humility, open-mindedness, and an awareness of the need for the Holy Spirit's activity in this decision-making process. "Lord guide us into all truth" wasn't far from their lips. Just like the men at the Jerusalem Council, they recognized the Holy Spirit as active in leading them into a unified decision, as well as being active in the actual decision itself. That's Luke's point when he said in Acts 15: 28, "It seemed best to the Holy Spirit and us."

The elders searched the Scriptures personally and deliberated collectively. They read several evangelical and scholarly books on the subject from evangelical Bible scholars who held to the inerrancy of Scripture and yet came to different positions on the biblical role of women in ministry. In reading and listening to the broad range of positions taken on it by good and godly people within the evangelical spectrum, our elders concluded there was no "right and wrong," and it was anything but "clear." They continued to try to understand what the text meant by inviting several Dallas Theological Seminary professors to elder meetings to share their knowledge. All three professors concluded, coming to their conclusion from different viewpoints, but concluded nonetheless that women could preach from the pulpit as long as she was under the authority of the elders. An interesting conclusion, considering anyone—male or female—who preaches in a pulpit should be under the authority of the leadership of the church!

I attended several of those discussions, but the last one sticks in my mind. A professor, whose church heritage was very conservative, where women wore head coverings and didn't speak in church, stated he could find no biblical reason why a woman couldn't preach under the authority of the elders. But just after the professor left, one of the elders turned to me and said, "Now will you [women] be satisfied?" This took me aback, reminding me of what we said to former slaves after emancipation. But I knew this man, and I knew his heart wasn't ugly. In fact I knew all of these elders came from conservative backgrounds, and yet they were courageously willing to tackle a difficult issue. Saying *yes* to a woman preaching was as far as they could go, and I respected them for it. But if I was honest, I knew it wasn't the end of the conversation. We had not even broached the issue of eldership or the roles in the home.

"If you're asking if this conversation is done," I said, "the answer is no. In about five years you will have someone insisting you tackle the issue of elder-ship and the home."

It got quiet.

Our elder board was a bit unique in that they didn't take a vote but rather they conversed until they felt unified in their decision. A year-and-a-half after the start of their inquiry, they came to a unified decision. In light of the teaching of Scripture, the leadership of the Holy Spirit, and the state of the culture they were attempting to reach for Christ and his Kingdom, it "seemed good to them" for women to preach from the pulpit under the authority of the elders. [55]

---

55   Their key conclusions follow: The accounts of creation and the fall (Genesis 1–3) reveal a fundamental equality between men and women; women exercised significant ministry roles of teaching and leading with God's blessing in both Old and New Testaments; though the role of women was historically limited, the progress of revelation indicates an ethic in progress leading to full freedom for women to exercise their giftedness in the local church; key New Testament passages restricting women's roles were cultur-ally and historically specific, not universal principles for all time and places, and though women are free to use all of their giftedness in teaching and leading in the church, the role of elder seems to be biblically relegated to men. The full 24-page decision can be found online at: www.irvingbible.org/fileadmin/site_files/adults/women/women_ministry_IBC.pdf

I need to say: though the elders were unified, they were not in complete agreement. One elder didn't feel comfortable with the decision. However, he did not let his view hold back the rest of the board from their position. That particular elder continued to attend the church even after they implemented the decision, though he chose not to attend service when a woman preached. I appreciated his compromise and commitment in being Christians together. It seems this was the goal at the Jerusalem Council, and this man depicted that truth beautifully.

Rolling out a new policy like this is a big deal for a church. Our leadership did some things well and some—well, not so well. But we all know hindsight is 20/20. For the first step, the elders gathered all staff, spouses and significant lay leaders in the church. The elders shared their year-and-a-half long journey and their conclusion that women could preach under the authority of the elders. Although their inquiry into the issue had not been public, it had not been a secret either. Most of the staff was aware of the conversation and were not surprised by their conclusion. The bigger concern for the staff was "how will this impact us?" rather than "I don't agree with this."

Though none of the staff left their jobs because of the decision, some did take a "beating" from their extended family members and or friends who were concerned the church had gone "liberal." These caught us all by surprise. And though we had anticipated push-back from the church, none of us expected the whipping we were about to receive from our brothers and sisters in the Dallas Fort Worth area and beyond.

The next step began with two town hall meetings held in the Irving Bible Church's "town square." The congregation was invited to hear from the elders and ask questions. At the end of the gatherings, people were encouraged to attend several upcoming workshops at the church. Dr. Barry Jones, a professor at Dallas Theological Seminary, and Pastor Andy, led those workshops. Both Pastor Andy and Dr. Jones went over the Scriptures in question and gave a synopsis of the 24-page position paper on the role of women. Then they opened the floor to questions. There were few adversarial comments or questions.

In the end, though we did lose several families due to our elders' decision, the majority of church members were not rocked by their decision. We had ripples, but no tidal waves. Clearly, the Holy Spirit had been at work in the hearts and minds of the congregants. Many churches split over the women's issue, we did not.

However, one of the families who did leave was that of my closest friend. When Kellie told me they were leaving because they could no longer "get behind the leadership," I felt the tidal wave I thought we'd avoided crash down on me.

Though Kellie handled the conflict graciously, reminding me it wasn't personal, at the time, I didn't know how to separate the job from the person. My husband, Steve, *was* the leadership. Heck, *I* was the leadership. I found myself in a weird place—having to navigate a friendship with such opposing views. Views that had everything to do with my profession. Losing that friendship devastated me. Looking back, I came to see the importance of not letting theology divide friendship.

Pastors and pastors' wives are lonely and isolated people. It's difficult to let others in, knowing things you say can be used against you or your mate somewhere down the line. It sounds paranoid, but it happens. And it happens a lot. When we first entered the ministry, Steve and I attended a Galatians 6:6 retreat for pastors and their wives. Though we were the youngest in the group by about thirty years, the death-like atmosphere in the room had little to do with age. One instructor shared a story of a woman coming to him for counseling. She looked so worn and terrified that the counselor suspected she'd been raped. His next question was, "Oh, are you a pastor's wife?" And indeed, she was. Caution! Being a pastor's wife can be hazardous to your health. [56]

I had worked so hard to have a kindred friend, a cherished friend whom I'd found in Kellie, and now she was leaving—over a theological difference.

---

56   Pastors and their families tend to have more physical ailments than the general population. These physical problems are primarily stress-induced illnesses or physical maladies associated with stress.
www.uu.edu/centers/rglee/fellows/spring03/kissell.htm, April 2015

Following Jesus is a journey, but once again I was discovering, choosing to follow Jesus—no matter what—is costly.

But I followed Jesus to that pulpit. While attending the National Pastor's Conference Pastor Andy *informed* (notice: he didn't ask) me I was going to be the first female preacher up at IBC. Immediately I said, "What about Jill Briscoe? She's done this before. Let her go first."

"No," Pastor Andy said. "It needs to be a woman that our church knows."

"What about Sue [Dr. Sue Edwards, my predecessor at IBC]? She's older than me. She's lived longer. She's closer to death. Let her go first!"

I didn't want to be the sacrificial lamb here!

But the answer was: "You need to be the one."

I've always pictured a dinner table when reading Paul's statement in Galatians 3:28: "There is no longer Jew or Gentile, slave or free, male and female. For you are all one in Christ Jesus."

Can you imagine these people groups sitting down together for a "family" meal (the text indicates they are one in Christ, family, right)? Can you see the slave sitting next to the master and the master looking over like, "Hey, can you get me a drink?" and the slave going, "Nah. I'm off duty while sitting here."

There's awkwardness, rolling of the eyes, confusion, irritation expressed through body language. I think that's what happens to the church when a decision like IBC's is rolled out. Rolling the eyes. Awkwardness. Confusion. It takes time for these groups to meld into a family, into a new way of living with each other. After all, the new paradigm was unheard of—un-thought of.

I knew a woman preaching at IBC would be somewhat like pulling up to that dinner table. It would take time. It would take rethinking, reliving. I didn't want to be the one, but truth is I knew someone had to do it. Someone needed to fill in the gap in the line. People are dying, living in hell and headed straight there. And we, the church can't afford to have any gaps. Not a one. All must step up. Lives depend on it.

So I stood up and preached from the pulpit.

Chapter Seven

SERMONS, SIRENS AND SALADS

"ONE, IF BY land, and two, if by sea" references the secret signal orchestrated by Paul Revere's historic ride from Boston to Concord to alert patriots about the advancement of the British troops. Just before I preached my first sermon at Irving Bible Church, a pastor in Denton (a city just north of Irving) sounded a similar alarm. His letter[57] alerted other evangelical pastors in the Dallas-Fort Worth area about the liberalism advancing within a neighboring church: Irving Bible Church.

> *June 4, 2008*
> Dear Pastor,
>
> I've pastored for 31 years in Denton and have never had a reason to contact other pastors with what Denton Bible was doing—until now. We are doing a three-week series at DBC on the egalitarian issue, "Can a woman be in authority over a man in the local church?" "Can they serve as pastors, elders or deacons over a man?"

---

57   jimhamilton.info/2008/06/05/denton-bible-holding-the-line/

The *teaching* of the Bible is "no" (I Tim. 2:9–15; 1 Cor. 14:34);

The *example* of the Bible is that men lead;

The *historic position* of the church is that men lead;

Because of these, this has been our position at DBC.

In the last 20 years this has been challenged. Even within my own seminary—Dallas Theological Seminary—this has been challenged…

May God equip you in every good thing to do his will.

Tom Nelson,

Senior Pastor

Reverend Nelson acknowledged to the *Dallas Morning News* that "his church's sermon series on the Bible and gender roles came in part because of Irving Bible Church's conclusion about women and preaching."

Unfortunately, my evangelical brothers (and sisters) weren't the only ones to hear the alarm.

The Friday before I preached for the first time, I received a call from a reporter at *The Dallas Morning News.* Sam Hodges had captured Rev. Nelson's perspective (*"…his friends in Irving are on 'dangerous' ground." Rev. Nelson said. "If the Bible is not true and authoritative on the roles of men and women, then maybe the Bible will not be finally true on premarital sex, the homosexual issue, adultery or any other moral issue. I believe this issue is the carrier of a virus by which liberalism will enter the evangelical church…* "[58]) and now he wanted mine.

I told him I'd have to get back to him. As I hung up I thought, *What if something I say is misquoted or taken out of context? What if I say something stupid? What if I get offended and respond in a way that does damage to the church? Or Christ?*

I called my husband and Pastor Andy. "Should I do this?" I asked.

"Yes," both said.

---

58   wfaa.com/story/news/local/2014/08/06/13426552/ April 2015

I haven't always found our calling to submit to one another[59] easy. But a "yes" answer from both my husband and my pastor made it clear that God wanted me to put aside my un-ease and submit to their wisdom.

———

On August 23rd the headlines of the religious section of *The Dallas Morning News* read: "Woman's turn in the pulpit at Irving Bible Church generates buzz, beefs." The article captured the elders' journey, their key points, the controversy with Reverend Nelson's letter as well as the news that Dr. Mark Bailey, president of Dallas Theological Seminary, was leaving Irving Bible Church.

Sam Hodges wrote in his *Dallas Morning News* piece: "The Dallas seminary, which supplies pastors to Bible churches around the country, has long had close ties with Irving Bible Church. But Dr. Bailey said that he and his wife, Barby, were amicably distancing themselves for "personal convictions and professional reasons."[60]

Many on the blogosphere took Dr. Bailey's departure as a rejection of IBC and therefore a win for their stance against our position. I'm not convinced that was so. I've often wondered if the outcome would have been different if the warning sirens hadn't been so public. What I do know is Dr. Bailey had a very amicable relationship with us. Dr. Bailey wrote an article for Dallas Theological Seminary's magazine to give clarity to Hodge's article. In it, Dr. Bailey shared his appreciation for our church along with the gracious withdrawal letter he sent to Pastor Andy.[61]

July 1, 2008
Dear Andy:

Because of my position at the seminary and the potential for mis-understandings and misperceptions that may arise by my "official" involvement as a part of the speaker team at IBC, after much prayer

---

59   See Ephesians 5:21 and James 4:7

60   wfaa.com/story/news/local/2014/08/06/13426552 April 2015

61   dts.edu/read/a-note-of-clarification-concerning-the-dallas-news-article-8-23-08/

and deliberation, it would seem prudent for me to step away from that role. Andy, you along with the IBC staff and elders have sought to be transparent, humble, and honest at every turn. As you no doubt understand there remains some ambiguity and uncertainty as to where the women in the ministry issues will lead.

As I mentioned to you, our appreciation for IBC as a church and for your ministry as a pastor is immense. We are committed to not being a source of contention or schism. We will quietly recede and not speak evil of anyone. For both personal convictions and professional reasons of keeping our alignment with the seminary position unquestioned, we believe before God that such a decision is warranted at this time.

… I am committed to fostering the great relationship DTS and IBC have sustained over the years…

With much affection for you, my friend,

Mark and Barby

In the article, Dr. Bailey summarized the seminary's position on the role of men and women. He wrote:

Students, staff, and constituents of Dallas Seminary inquire at times about the Seminary's position concerning the roles of men and women in the Seminary and in Christian ministry in general. On many questions raised, the Seminary has taken no official position and faculty members have no consensus. However, *Dallas Theological Seminary does hold the position that the Scriptures limit the roles of the local church elder and senior pastor to men* (emphasis mine).

Interestingly enough, even though we reached our conclusion[62] differently than Dallas Theological Seminary reached theirs, the conclusions are

---

62   IBC and DTS differed on "…an ethic in progress leading to full freedom for women to exercise their giftedness in the local church."

similar. Both IBC and DTS restricted women from the role of elder or senior pastor but neither restricted a woman from preaching in the pulpit *under the authority of the elders.* Yet from what many people read, our views were night and day.

Though as I prepared for my first-time in the pulpit at Irving Bible, to my surprise, I discovered the controversy was not forefront on everyone's mind. As I soon discovered, my *hair* and what I'd *wear* were of utmost concern to many in my midst.

"Wear your hair up," some suggested. "It's less wild, more professional."

"Remember: No cleavage!" others warned me. "Wear a jacket to cover your breasts."

"And wear *long* pants. No ankle length," I was told. "But be sure they aren't too tight."

We all grow up learning how to "dress for success," but the message I received was over the top.

Why was everyone so worried about my appearance? Did the men who visited our pulpit receive such concern? I doubted it.

I suspected there were several things at play. First, I was first. My hitting it out of the "ballpark"—in everything from my message to my appearance— meant a win for all of womankind. Not hitting it out of the park would confirm what Augustine taught: that "women can't bring it."

Second, because I was a woman, some worried my appearance might cause men to stumble. (Remember: women are temptresses, right?). In my training, I had learned preaching is truth poured out through personality. But with each warning over how I'd dress, I was told that some men would not hear the truth because of my *sexuality.* Whereas my appearance matters in preaching as it helps communicate my personality, more importantly, the body is the location in which *spirituality* is lived out. Not just *sexuality.* Living as kingdom people means we recognize that in God's Kingdom women are to be realized as fully human and not simply reduced to our sexual parts.[63] This is the point this female theologian is making:

> We had gathered to hear an eminent theologian speak about her new book, and as I glanced around, I estimated that the room was at least 80 percent male—a mix of old and young in tweed, shiny loafers, and dress shirts. When the theologian rose from a chair in the front row and moved to the podium, I almost audibly gasped. She was wearing a tight black dress and a short red jacket. The dress was cut so low that the tops of her breasts appeared.
>
> ...The woman in question was not young, maybe twenty years older than I am. She was attractive, but not conventionally beautiful. She had spent more of her life in libraries doing close readings of church fathers. Her works were weighty and sometimes luminous...Here she was in front of me, arguing earnestly, sifting through her readings of Augustine, skillfully maneuvering the objections raised to her work, deftly answering questions. I continued to stare, mesmerized. Did she know what she was doing? A ridiculous question: she seemed to know not only her own mind, but also to be reading the minds of everyone else in the room. I couldn't help but think that she had calculated how much of her breasts to show as carefully as she had chosen which passages of Thomas Aquinas to quote. *She was offering this dress in this moment as a challenge, as yet another dare: She was risking a fully female theological incarnation...*
>
> Her cleavage was calculated—that I know almost for certain.

---

63   "This is not to say that women (and men) are to slather around as sexually charged exhibitionists. What I am saying is that women must not have our sexual nature held responsible for a man's sexual nature. This not only shames women, but it shames men. It creates an image of men as being unable (and irresponsible) to control themselves, that men cannot be trusted with women, nor women with men. This leads to the separation and isolation of the sexes from one another..." Pam Hogeweide, *Unlady Like: Resisting the Injustice of Inequality in the Church* (Civitas Press, 2012) p. 57.

She showed just enough that no one could mistake it…. But not so much that it could be called distasteful… There was nothing flirtatious in it. That is perhaps what made the gesture still more remarkable. Her cleavage, I decided, was a subtle mark, a distinct challenge to Christianity's usual ways of speaking, a gesture in the direction of the unsay-able. *She rejected the bargain that the rest of us seemed to have struck: that we would leave our bodies outside the room. That we would be sexless in order to be taken seriously.* Maybe the women would add a dash of the "feminine" in the form, usually a scarf, a pair of glittery earrings, a shade of lipstick, so that femininity could act as an assessory to the endless parade of gray suits, a flair, a touch, but never the real thing itself, the female body…

◇——————◇
"MY EMBODIED SELF IS NOT TO BE FEARED."
◇——————◇

…I heard this theologian saying, but not in so many words; *"You will not separate my work from my body; my body and my work are one with my being and with my soul. I offer them to you together."* That's an earnest version. *The less earnest would be, "I will not show up here bodiless so that you can feel safe in your Empire of the Tweed-Suited Mind"*[64] (emphasis mine).

The Sunday morning I preached my first sermon at Irving Bible Church, I did not wear a tight black dress, nor did I cloak my gender in a tweed suit. God's truth demands we not live as dualists. We are not to disguise nor deny nor live separate from our body. I am an embodied female, a part of God's blessed alliance, a part of the link in the chain, and my embodied self is not to be feared.

---

64   Amy Frykholm, "Going in Disguise," *Talking Taboo* (White Cloud Press, 2013) pp. 3–5.

—

Sunday morning had arrived. Just after breakfast, the phone rang. On the other end, a woman with a British accent asked: "Are you sure? Are you sure you are good before God? You must be sure."

Jill Briscoe knew all too well the punches thrown at female preachers. She shared of a time when the president of a prestigious Bible college invited her to speak. During her time on stage, some men in the audience turned their backs in protest to a woman speaking in front of men. Jill was one of the women who had forged a path for those of us coming behind.

"Yes," I told her. "I am sure. God has given me the right, privilege, and gifting to preach."

I didn't see it then as clearly as I do now, but God had prepared me. God had taught me to weather these trials and push forward. Ever since I had bent over and planted seeds one at a time, he had been preparing me for such a time as this.

We serve God whether people honor us or despise us whether they slander us or praise us, 2 Corinthians 6:8 tells us.

"But," I told Jill, "I'm afraid; afraid I won't handle myself well."

Oh, I wasn't afraid of preaching. I knew how to preach. I was afraid of what might happen off stage—particularly if a combative person approached me. *What if I make my church look bad—or worse yet, Jesus?*

Jill's advice was invaluable. She said there would be small and large offenses to forgive. But I'm not Christ—only he can forgive everyone all at once. I would have to forgive one offense at a time. And yes, there would be times I'd be approached and my response would be anything but admirable. There would be times I would simply say, "Shut up" (as Jill had, supposedly, with her beautiful British accent) and walk away.

"You won't be perfect," Jill told me. "Only Jesus is that."

Her words to me that morning were like someone releasing air from an overfilled bicycle tire. Just a little air—pssss—let out, enough so the tire wouldn't pop.

That Sunday, August 24, at the nine o'clock service, I sat in the front row between Pastor Andy and Bryan, my bodyguard. Family and friends sat in the row behind us. (One particular friend who showed up to all three services had been strongly advised by her senior pastor to "stay home" and not show support by attending.) They sat there at the nine o'clock, again at the eleven o'clock, and again at the five o'clock service.

With the room packed and the Channel 8 News cameras rolling, Pastor Andy stood and explained IBC's journey. Then he asked the audience to welcome the first woman to preach in our church's forty-year history. To my surprise the audience applauded.

Before walking up to the stage, I turned to my daughter to let her know that just like Jill had chopped a few vines, so too was I about to chop a few to forge a path for her generation. She knew what I meant. She knew I meant something beyond a woman preaching from the pulpit. Madison knew I believed God was moving—globally—to address the gender injustice of women. Whether it was covert gender injustice like what goes on in the American church, or overt gender injustice like what we see in sex trafficking or in female genital mutilation, or the myriad other forms of female oppression, God was calling out what happens to his women and girls around the world. Madison knew I didn't view women preaching from the pulpit as "the issue," but rather a byproduct of what God was really doing: recreating humanity as he originally intended.

I so firmly believed God was up to something on behalf of his daughters, Madison included, that I was willing to serve him "whether people honored me or despised me whether they slandered me or praised me" (2 Corinthians 6:8). I had received God's unconditional, without-limits love, and I wasn't backing down from serving him no matter what. I love the way Erwin McManus says it in, *The Barbarian Way:*[65]

---

65   *The Barbarian Way* is one of my top ten books. Being a Barbarian Christian means to "fight for the heart of our King," - no matter what. I took it so seriously I had "barbarian" tattooed on my wrist.

When we turn our hearts toward God all of our fears are consumed by one fear. We are called to fear only God. There is an important reason for this. What we fear is what we're subject to; our fears define our master. Where there is no fear, there is no control. When we fear God and God only, we are no longer bound by all of the other fears that would hold us captive. The fear of death, the fear of failure, the fear of rejection, the fear of insignificance – all the fears that know us by name and haunt us in the dark of the night become powerless when we know the fear of the Lord.[66]

I stood up—heart racing, adrenaline pumping—and walked to the podium. Under my breath, I prayed, "Jesus speak." And then I did what I had done so many times before: I preached the Word of God to God's people. The passage was from John 4, Samaritan Woman, the title so fitting: "Fight for the Heart of our King."

After the service, I came off the stage and stood to receive the line of people. Some wanted prayer, others to lend support, and others to simply say hello. Everyone who approached was gracious. Even still, it was comforting to have Bryan's looming stature standing beside me.

A tall, elegant woman stood in line waiting to speak. When she approached I offered my hand and asked, "Do I know you? You look so familiar."

"No," she said. "But you know my daddy, Dr. Haddon Robison. He called and said one of his students was speaking and asked if I would attend."

At the end of each service there was a line of gracious men and women. Unfortunately, that wasn't true of the blogosphere.

Betty Friedan, author and feminist activist accurately said, "Change has always been threatening to the keepers of the status quo."[67] The change at IBC stirred, even threatened, those who held the "traditional" view on the role of women. The blogosphere sounded the alarm with statements like:

---

66   Erwin McManus, *The Barbarian Way* (Nashville, Thomas Nelson, 2005) p. 101.

67   Betty Friedan, Betty, *Life So Far* (New York: Simon & Schuster, 2006) p. 211.

"Grave moral concern"

"Cancer to the Church"

"Slippery slope to liberalism"

"Dangerous"

People said:

" ...When my 4 month-old son is my age, I doubt if IBC will have a shred of orthodox teaching."

Steve and I were called the "power couple" (aiming to be the power couple from the beginning).

I was a "b****" (rhymes with witch).

Another blogger made the correlation that my preaching would lead to bestiality. (All I could do was laugh at that one!)

One young female seminarian said if her mother knew she was at my Bible study, her mom would say she was with the antichrist.

Many times I chuckled at the comments, but it was a cover up. It hurt to have others—most of whom were anonymous—say such ugly things about me, my husband, and our church. As the week went on, I became deeply troubled. (I'm still deeply troubled, actually, by the way we Christians treat one another.) I was troubled that people who didn't know me or my heart or my calling attacked me in public, that they put Christ's reputation on display through his people—and that non-Christians were reading.

My extended family, many of whom aren't believers, were reading. My older brother asked: "What the *hell* is going on down there? Do I need to come down there and kick some ass?"

My heart was troubled. Why would my brother want our Jesus if this was what Jesus people were like?

Scot McKnight challenges this brutal treatment within our ranks:

We are all into being "right" and at times theologians have been brutal while showing they were right... there's a difference between focusing on being right and focusing on being a follower of Jesus. For Jesus,

everything is shaped toward becoming people who love God and who
love others, and nothing less than a life absorbed in love is sufficient to
describe what a Christian is for him.[68]

The anonymous and disconnected cyberspace made it easier for people to debate and mock without any accountability. I wondered how different the dialogue would have been had we been incarnate, face-to-face conversation with one another.

Hurtful as it was, day after day I scanned the blogs like an addict. The Counsel for Biblical Manhood and Womanhood had issued a statement. Denny Burk, Professor of Biblical Studies at Boyce College, wrote a blog post. Later he took Pastor Andy to task on the radio.[69]

All the while, I received encouraging emails from professors, friends, and fellow colleagues in ministry. The whole thing was bizarre. I kept thinking, "Isn't there something more important for all of us to be talking about?" But I kept reading the good and the bad notes, all the while. Finally Steve stepped in.

"No more reading blogs or emails," he said. "It's too upsetting. It's not healthy for you."

He was right. So I stopped listening—to the critics *and* the praise.

—

I had once sat across from our men's minister as he explained Dr. Robert Lewis' "Four Faces of Manhood," which are King, Warrior, Lover and Friend. I'm not comfortable with stringent categories, especially as I believe women—whether light pink or lime green or anything between or beyond—can obtain these characteristics also. Just after I preached at IBC, Warrior Jackie showed up. Especially when my kids got roped into the criticism. Something that's *not* okay with mama. You don't believe women are warriors? Well, just go after their kids (or husband) and look out.

---

68   Scot McKnight, *One Life* (Grand Rapids, Mich.: Zondervan, 2010) p. 47.

69   www.dennyburk.com/radio-debate-with-the-pastor-of-ibc/

Once, my daughter Madison was getting a ride home with a friend. Her mom was waiting in the carpool line for another child when a woman approached the car. She leaned into the driver's side window and started talking about the "IBC thing." She was unaware that my daughter was sitting in the back seat. Madison, who is quiet and private, slumped down, hoping not to be noticed. Then there was Hunter's friend—a boy who had spent hours and hours at our house—who felt the IBC decision was a sin. His parents agreed and he told Hunter. They argued, and I could tell from Hunter's expression it hurt. No child should be told their mother is a sinner for preaching God's Word to God's people.

But in the midst of this, I found an outlet, a refuge in the kitchen, of all places. I began to create amazing salads. (My favorite being beets with goat cheese, arugula with Parmesan, kale with tomatoes and quinoa with mint, almonds and cranberries. For the recipe, see the end of the chapter).

Looking back, I realize I focused on cooking after I started preaching because I was afraid to go out to eat. I didn't want to be approached—or worse—accosted. It wasn't an unfounded fear. Our close friends Ben and Amy had invited Steve and me to dinner. We walked into the quaint restaurant to see them standing talking to two other couples, who had attended church with them years back. The aisle was tight, so Steve walked in front of me. Ben introduced Steve as he approached the two couples. They shook hands and just then I appeared from behind Steve, Ben continued his introductions. The man closest to me put out his hand to shake hello. But then he heard my name and saw my face (the face he saw on the news and the paper), and he pulled his hand away and stepped back.

The sirens had rung: "One, if by land, and two, if by sea."

So I learned to make great salads.

INGREDIENTS:

2 cups chicken broth

1 cup quinoa

3 tablespoons olive oil

½ cup coarsely chopped mint leaves

½ cup dry-roasted almonds, unsalted

½ cup dried cranberries

1 cup coarsely chopped kale

½ cup sliced carrots

½ cup sliced celery

1 scallion, thinly sliced

18 grape tomatoes, halved

1 lemon, juiced

½ teaspoon lemon zest

Salt and ground black pepper to taste

DIRECTIONS:

1. Bring the chicken broth to a boil in a saucepan over high heat. Add quinoa, reduce heat to medium-low, cover, and simmer until the quinoa is tender and the liquid has been absorbed, about 13 minutes. Stir in olive oil; fluff quinoa with a fork. Set aside to cool slightly.

2. Stir mint, almonds, dried cranberries, kale, carrots, celery, scallion, grape tomatoes, lemon juice, and lemon zest. Season to taste with salt and ground black pepper.

Chapter Eight

IT'S A GOSPEL ISSUE

"ARE YOU AN egalitarian?"

My face flushed at the question.

For several years I had been invited to speak at the All About Influence Conference at Dallas Theological Seminary. That is, until 2008. Then all I got was silence. It hurt. To get silence from an institution that deeply transformed my life felt like a father's rejection. I had accepted this was one of the consequences for saying yes to preaching at IBC—until 2014, that is, when their conference brochure arrived in the mail advertising three women speakers I had trained. Perhaps the ice had thawed, I thought. So I inquired about the possibility of selling my book *She Can Teach: Empowering Women to Teach the Scriptures Effectively* at their women's conference.

I was met with the question: "Are you an egalitarian?"

Carolyn Custis James is correct when she says, "Are you a complementarian or egalitarian?" has become the litmus test—a modern day shibboleth to determine whether a woman is orthodox or heretical, safe or dangerous. Women are routinely pressed to declare where their loyalties lie, and when they do declare themselves, it can cause estrangement."[70]

---

70   James, Carolyn Custis, Half the Church, 154.

This should not be surprising to us. Newness comes at a price. In *Simply Good News*, N.T. Wright writes: "Jesus himself saw that his good news would be bad news to people who had invested heavily in the old ways. Plenty of people looked at him and said he was crazy. Plenty more said he was dangerous… Jesus saw this opposition, this suspicion and hostility, as part of the deal. He had to come to set people free, and like Moses with Pharaoh, the king of Egypt, he was confronting the powers that held people captive."[71]

The position one holds on the role of women is not the litmus test for orthodoxy. The test should be the Gospel. Is this woman gospel-ing? Does the organization for which she works herald the Gospel? Jesus should always be our focal point. His person and work should trump our debates.

Perhaps because I believe this, I've been noodling this question: "Does the Gospel have anything to say about how men and women live, love, and work together?"

Actually, I think it's all about the Gospel.

So we have to do some thinking about what the Gospel is and how the Good News impacts women. For many the word *Gospel* means forgiveness of sins [72]—and that's true. But the original audience of the Gospels would have put that truth in a broader context.

For example, when Mark opened his Gospel with, "This is the Good News, Jesus the Messiah,[73] Son of God" his audience wouldn't immediately think "Jesus Christ died on the cross for our sins." Rather, they *would have* associated those terms with a king and his kingdom. See, they lived in a time

---

71   N.T. Wright, *Simply Good News* (San Francisco: HarperOne, 2015) p. 142.

72   1 Corinthians 15:3–4 explains the Good News as, "Christ died for our sins, just as Scriptures said. He was buried and was raised from the dead on the third day, just as Scriptures said. Romans 5: 8&10 states, "God shows his love for us in that while we were still sinners, Christ died for us" and "while we were enemies we were reconciled to God by the death of his Son, much more, now that we are reconciled, shall we be saved by his life."

73   Messiah (or Christ) means "anointed one" an anointed person is a person who has been nominated, appointed, chosen to do a particular task. Jesus was appointed King—his task was to bring about God's Kingdom.

when a herald stood in the city square to announce the birth of the king's son or a king's victory over an enemy such as when Octavian Augustus had victory over Mark Antony. "The Good News of the victory of..." The Good News was an announcement that "something had happened (or was happening) and as a result of which the world would become a different place."[74] This is how Mark's audience would have understood the term Good News. And all throughout the Gospels, Jesus is identified as a king[75]—a different kind of king, with a different kind of power—creating a different kind of people (kingdom people).

This is the point Jesus made when James and John requested the best seats in the palace.

> "You don't know what you are asking," Jesus said. "Can you drink
> the cup I drink or be baptized with the baptism I am baptized
> with?"
> "We can," they answered.
> Jesus said to them, "You will drink the cup I drink and be baptized
> with the baptism I am baptized with, but to sit at my right or left
> is not for me to grant. These places belong to those for whom they
> have been prepared."
> When the ten heard about this, they became indignant with James
> and John. Jesus called them together and said, "You know that
> those who are regarded as rulers of the Gentiles lord it over them,
> and their high officials exercise authority over them. Not so with
> you. *Instead, whoever wants to become great among you must be your
> servant, and whoever wants to be first must be slave of all* (Italics mine.
> Mark 10:38–44, NLT).

---

74   Wright, 77

75   The rest of Mark's Gospel demonstrates Jesus is King bringing in God's kingdom. He quoted Isaiah 40:3 (and Malachi 3:1) a passage that speaks of clearing rocks out of the road so a king could travel, then he described Jesus' baptism as if it was a king's coronation, then Jesus himself announced, "The Kingdom of God is near! Repent of your sins and believe the Good News" (Mark 1: 14–15).

Imagine the "huh?" look on the disciples' faces. This is not how royalty worked in their world.

Then in Luke 4:18–19, Jesus proclaims what his reign will accomplish: "The Spirit of the LORD is upon me, for he has anointed me to bring Good News to the poor. [God] has sent me to proclaim that captives will be released, that the blind will see, that the oppressed will be set free, and that the time of the LORD'S favor has come."

"The Lord's favor" is an allusion to the year of the Jubilee spoken of in the book of Leviticus. Basically, every fifty years, all debts were to be forgiven, slaves were to be given their freedom and ancestral lands were to be given back to their original family. The year of Jubilee was all about cancellation of debt and new beginnings. King Jesus had arrived to bring forgiveness, restoration, and transformation to God's creation. To recreate what God created in the beginning. To restore it back. To make it anew.

Paul said it like this: "Therefore, if anyone is in Christ, the new creation has come. The old has gone; the new is here" (2 Corinthians 5:17).

When we hear Paul's words, we need to think beyond the individual because Jesus' death and resurrection created a way for all creation to be put right again. N. T. Wright writes:

> Humans were the linchpins of his plan for how creation would
> flourish. We imagined the problem to be that we were out of touch
> with God and we needed to reestablish a relationship with him.
> Well, that is all true, but it's not the whole truth. We forget what
> humans (so to speak) were there for in the first place. God made
> humans so that he could look after his world through this particular
> creature. His intention was to bring his creation forward from its
> beginnings to be the glorious place he always intended and to do so
> through this human family… Creation was supposed to be brought
> to flourishing harmony, to a fruitful fulfillment, through the work
> of humans. So creation itself is frustrated, all because humans got it

wrong. The problem is not "Oh dear, humans sinned, so the whole creation will fail to attain its proper goal." ... The good news, therefore, is that when humans are put right the project can get back on track. Not all at once, of course, just as we humans are not put right completely and forever at a stroke. But this is the goal.[76]

This calling out a people to care for his earth and each other in loving sustainable ways isn't new. Remember that's what Man and Woman were commanded to do in the Garden? Then in Exodus 19, we see God call out the nation of Israel. Now, through Christ, we have a new people being called forth to carry out God's original design for humankind. Paul said this twist of events, where King Jesus died and got up and sent the Holy Spirit to unite adversarial people into one family was a "mysterious plan." To quote, "A message kept secret for centuries and generations has now been revealed to God's people.[77] For God wanted them to know that the riches and glory of Christ are for you Gentiles too. And this is the secret; Christ lives in you. This gives you assurance of sharing his glory" (Colossians 1:26- 27).

Kingdom people were put right so the project could get back on track. But, what can I say? They didn't get along very well. They didn't see each other as equals or valuable. Whether it was due to ethnic or gender prejudices, class divides, social status or socio-economic, they didn't sit with each other at the table. As we examine Paul's words, imagine how difficult it must have been for these people to become one. To live together as a different kind

---

76   Wright, 97–98.

77   In Exodus 19 the Lord revealed himself to the Israelites. He said, "You have seen what I did to the Egyptians. You know how I carried you on eagles' wings and brought you to myself. Now if you will obey me and keep my covenant, you will be my own special treasure from among all the peoples on earth; for all the earth belongs to me. And you will be my kingdom of priests, my holy nation" (Exodus 19: 4–6). The Apostle Peter repeats something similar about those people who profess faith in Jesus: "For you are a chosen people. You are royal priests, a holy nation, God's very own possession. As a result, you can show others the goodness of God, for he called you out of the darkness into his wonderful light" (1 Peter 2:9).

of people under the leadership of King Jesus. Consider how their new status in Christ—equal, valuable, new creations—shattered their cultural norms in the following verses:

Ephesians 2:15–16: "[Jesus] made peace between Jews and Gentiles by creating in himself one new people from two groups. Together as one body, Christ reconciled both groups to God by means of his death on the cross, and our hostility toward each other was put to death."

Jews and Gentiles in the same family? Impossible, they hated each other. Masters and slaves at the same table? Not going to happen!

Colossians 3:11: "In this new life, it doesn't matter if you are a Jew or a Gentile, circumcised or uncircumcised, barbaric, or uncivilized, slave or free. Christ is all that matters, and he lives in all of us."

Can you imagine the slave pulling up a chair at the table and the Master giving him an order? There's that "huh?" look again! Or, male and female eating side by side? That just didn't happen!

Galatians 3: 28: "There is no longer Jew or Gentile, slave or free, male or female. For you are all one in Christ Jesus."

Some argue Paul is speaking about salvation in these texts. Even if Paul were, surely it's not all he's saying. The picture is glaring at us. These groups don't go together. And yet, in Christ they are one. The Gospel means something had happened (or was happening) and as a result the world would be different, not just for individuals but for a community. Jesus said this new people would live by a different ethic than the world. Instead of power, position, gender, ethnicity, or color being the order of the day, for God's people it would be love. King Jesus kind of love. This is what Jesus laid out in the beatitudes and what followed in Luke 6. It's what he said to his disciples in John 13:35: "By this all people will know that you are my disciples, if you have love for one another." Love would order God's people.

I wonder how women like Bilhah and Zilpah might have heard this Good News. We read their story in Genesis 30. All we know of them is they are concubines (slave girls who have no voice or choice) used as pawns between two sisters, Leah and Rachel. Imagine how they felt when they were told to have sex with Leah and Rachel's husband, Jacob. Or how they felt when their children were handed over to their female masters, Leah and Rachel. The

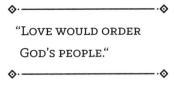

first time their birth children said "mama" would be to another woman. How would they hear Mark or Paul's words? Jesus' words? More than forgiveness of sins, they would have heard the Gospel and thought of a new way of living, have had hope for something beyond their "no voice, no choice" status. There was a bigger picture for them—the bigger picture Paul points toward.

We must wonder if Paul was also showing a trajectory toward true Kingdom living when he wrote the household codes in Ephesians 5:15–33 and Colossians 3:18–25. Before we go there, remember Paul wrote to these embryonic churches to help them figure out *how* to live this new Kingdom life while living as "resident aliens" in their communities. A gospel-ing kind of life *moves* people towards Kingdom living, a community where people live in "complete reconciliation, a state of the fullest flourishing in every dimension—physical, emotional, social, and spiritual—because all relationships are right, perfect, and filled with joy."[78] Does this sound idealistic? It should. It's how it was in the beginning and it's how it will be when King Jesus returns.

Paul took the Roman Empire's household codes—something from their culture—and shifted it toward truer Kingdom living. A trajectory. Below is the list of people involved in the household codes. Take note that those on the left have more power and authority than those on the right. The ones on the right are the more (if not the most) vulnerable in society:

Husband – Wife

Master – Slave

Father – Child

---

78   Tim Keller, *Generous Justice* (New York: Riverhead Books, 2012) p. 174.

On the left we have husband, master, father—all the same person: the man. On the right we have woman, servant, and child—three different people, all of whom are vulnerable to the man. In Ephesians, Paul started the codes by saying, "And further, submit to one another out of reverence for Christ…. For wives, this means submit to your husbands as to the Lord… For husbands, this means love your wives, just as Christ loved the church…" (Ephesians 5: 21–26).

Remarkable words in light of their culture where marriage was based on economics not love. Where men married women who perpetuated their public honor and continued an honorable bloodline. In a culture where women were more like property than person. In a culture where obedience was required, where the very idea of a man submitting to a wife was unheard of. Because submission is a choice. It's a voice.

Some argue Paul's household codes confirm some kind of creation order in the family. Man as leader of the household, woman as assistant. That conclusion leads us to think the Gospel is more about "cleaning up bad behaviors" in society than transforming it. Later in Ephesians, Paul writes, "A man leaves his father and mother and is joined to his wife, and the two are united into one. This is a *great mystery*, but it is an illustration of the way Christ and the church are one" (Ephesians 5:31–32, italics mine). Marriage is a mystery. Is it? Because what's so mysterious about a husband being a leader and a woman being his assistant? What if Paul was using a picture when he said man was the "head of wife"? What if it was a picture of oneness, where the husband's head is on his wife's body?

Imagine those tall plywood figures at a theme park or a carnival, where a person stands behind a goofy body and sticks her head through. One head on another's body. It's that kind of idea Paul wrote about. One yet two. Sound like anything else? The Trinity, three and one? Now that's a mystery. But I digress. The point is: the household codes are not affirmation of some kind of created order, but rather a movement towards something new.

Jesus said the Kingdom was near, meaning new creation has *begun* even though the Kingdom of God has not been fully realized—yet. It will be—in the new heavens and new earth (Revelation 19, 21–22). For now, we struggle toward that glorious future. The Scriptures and the Person of Jesus Christ have left us signposts pointing the way. But the journey down that road has been—and will continue to be—complicated, messy, and sometimes downright ugly.

This means: We will continue to have church splits over "the woman's issue." We'll have all-male leadership who exclude (intentionally but more than likely unintentionally) women from the table. Women's voices will remain limited, even though over half of church attendees are women. Women's gifts and service will, at times, be limited, devalued, and/or unseen. We will continue to live with a selective narrative where we are told the ideal biblical woman is light pink and we will find lime green women dangerous. We will ask the wrong questions and, at times, wrongly interpret the Scriptures. (And this doesn't even begin to speak to what's happening to women and girls around the globe due to beliefs that women aren't fully human.[79] There is a correlation between the theological stance a society takes on women and girls and the level of poverty and violence in that society. The more a society uses theological grounds to subjugate women and girls, the higher the poverty and violence levels will be in that society.[80]) But most of all, we will keep God's design for what Carolyn Custis James calls the "blessed alliance" from fully flourishing.

In 2011, I stepped down from my position at IBC to start The Marcella Project, a ministry committed to ennobling women through Scripture focused teaching, training, and dialogue. Our vision is to transform the way women view themselves and the way the church views women so that the

---

79   In 1979 a UN Convention was organized to give women rights, human rights, which should have been granted to them under the UN Human Rights Mandate. It appears that some countries did not assume women qualified as human. I wish I could say that idea vanished with time, but it hasn't. There are still areas in the world where women and girls are not seen as human.

80   Lisa Sharon Harper, "Shalom and Gender Justice," Sojourners blog, Sept 10, 2013, sojo.net/blogs/2013/09/10/shalom-and-gender-justice

church can get at what's happening to women and girls around the globe. One of the ways we transform the view of women is by hosting "salons," which are informed conversations around spiritual issues that impact women. At one of our most recent salons, "Can Men and Women Be Friends?" a male elder shared how prior to his church having elders they had leadership teams. Men and women were on those teams. "We were better when women were on the team," he said. "Now, we meet to discuss issues, come to a conclusion, go home talk with our wives, and realize there are many aspects we didn't take into account. So we have to have another meeting."

It was better when women were on the team. Whether this man agrees or disagrees with women as elders, he does recognize the need for the blessed alliance.

Recently, *Forbes* magazine ran an article stating, "Companies with higher female participation at board level exhibit higher returns and payout ratios."[81] The World Bank said women are the best investment for an economy. As Secretary of State, Hilary Clinton said women are our best foreign policy. Study after study[82] shows "...when women gain control over spending, less family money is devoted to instant gratification and more for education and starting small businesses."[83]

The world is starting to notice that families and cultures are healthier when women's voices are heard. The same is true for the family of God.

But again, it takes some rugged messiness to get there. Good thing we are not alone in the endeavor. Remember King Jesus. He's a different kind of king, with a different kind of power creating a different kind of people.

---

81   Karen Higginbottom, "More Women on the Board Means Higher Returns for Firms," *Forbes,* Oct. 10, 2014. forbes.com/sites/karenhigginbottom/2014/10/02/more-women-on-the-board-means-higher-returns-for-firms/

82   Viviana A. Zelizer, "The Gender of Money," *Wall Street Journal,* Jan. 27, 2011. blogs.wsj.com/ideas-market/2011/01/27/the-gender-of-money/ April 13, 2015

83   Sheryl WuDunn, *Half the Sky: Turning Oppression into Opportunity for Women Worldwide*goodreads.com/work/quotes/6444203-half-the-sky-turning-oppression-into-opportunity-for-women-worldwide

Paul spoke of this King Jesus' different kind of power: internal transformation instead of external rules, producing love—the new ethic.

Shortly after Paul got excited about God's mysterious plan of Jew and Gentile becoming one family he said, "For this reason, I pray that from his glorious, unlimited resources he will empower you with *inner strength through his Spirit.*" Another translation says it like this: "…that he would grant you… *to be strengthened with might by his Spirit in the inner man* (so) that Christ may dwell in your heart by faith" (Ephesians 3:14).

The Spirit using all his unlimited divine resources to empower our innermost being, our mind, will, and emotions, to love each other—especially across the deep racial, gender, and cultural divides that previously had separated us. In *The King Jesus Gospel,* Scot McKnight writes: "We no longer have to live under the conditions of the fall where we emphasized otherness but rather we can live under the conditions of the new creation, where the emphasis is oneness… People of the Spirit empowered by the Spirit to live in ways not attainable by ordinary means."[84]

> "PEOPLE OF THE SPIRIT EMPOWERED BY THE SPIRIT TO LIVE IN WAYS NOT ATTAINABLE BY ORDINARY MEANS."
>
> —SCOT MCKNIGHT

What we have going on in our churches and around the globe is not a women's issue; it's a human issue. It's not an issue about women's equality. Jesus didn't die so we could be equal. Jesus died for something bigger than that. Equality means I've got my rights, and you've got yours, and so we're good with each other. Do you hear how we can simply tolerate rather than integrate? Instead, God created man and woman (community) to live in *shalom.* Whenever and wherever shalom is broken, we hear the cry of our Savior, "I'm offended." That's bigger than equality. It may include equality, but it doesn't rest there.

---

84   Scot McKnight, *The King Jesus Gospel* (Grand Rapids, Mich.: Zondervan, 2011) p. 105

Interdependent. Intertwined. Embracing otherness, as we become oneness.

The American church is so caught up in the smaller issues, like whether or not a woman can or can't preach from a Sunday morning pulpit, that we've missed what God is really doing. He's moving to recreate humanity as he intended. And with what little I understand, I do know God will have his way. With or without us, he will get it done. My prayer for us is that we would not miss what he's doing because we are so caught up in the smaller things of life.

Is this gospel-ing? That's the question to be asked.

Chapter Nine

FOR WOMEN ONLY

As Dorothy sipped her coffee, she shared her love for her church, how's she's been a member for a long time and doesn't want to leave, but how she's not sure how to reconcile her feelings with their tightened stance on what women may and may not do in her church. Dorothy is not light pink. You could say she's more like scarlet purple. She's in her fifties, never been married, has no children, and she works in corporate America. She's been a successful leader in her workplace, but as we sipped our lattes she confessed she'd always dreamed of being a pastor.[85] She knew that would never be. She's female after all. She'd accepted that being a pastor was out of her reach, but the more her pastor talked about the limitations for women, the more disturbed she'd become. Dorothy was experiencing what many of us women experience at some point—that our gender is a liability.

What should she do?

Sitting with women like Dorothy has become commonplace. At every retreat, conference, bible study, training, or salon, there's a woman (or two or three) who pull me aside to share a similar story. These women are hurt

---

85   It can be argued that a pastor can be the spiritual gift and or an office. Ephesians 4:8–11 strivetoenter.com/wim/2007/09/10/is-pastor-one-of-the-spiritual-gifts/

and confused. They long to be obedient to Jesus. My advice to women like Dorothy—and to all women who serve in conservative faith communities—is to be diligent in knowing what they know. Evangelicals demand biblical proof, therefore we must know what the Bible says and how it's been interpreted.[86] We don't have to be a scholar or attend seminary,[87] although I would argue some women should, but we do need to read different positions,[88] understand the arguments, and pray for clarity from the Spirit (John 16:13). We must know what we know.

But let me digress. As we learn, we must do so with a heart of love and humility. Jesus is our example. Consider the words of Philippians 2:1–5:

> Is there any encouragement from belonging to Christ? Any comfort from his love? Any fellowship together in the Spirit? Are your hearts tender and compassionate? Then make me truly happy by

---

86   When I attended the Evangelical Theological Society in San Francisco in 2011, only one percent of the presenters were women. I inquired as to why so few. One of the female professors commented that conservative evangelical seminaries only opened their doors to women in the 1970s. *It's taking time to catch up.* Seven hundred presenters, almost all were older white males of western decent. One has to wonder how the interpretation of Scripture has been impacted by that fact. We need more women in academia.

87   When I met Stacy she was the Director of Women at a megachurch in Arkansas. She had no formal training. A conversation ensued that changed all that. "Then I met Jackie Roese, a woman who at the time was completing her doctoral work in preaching, and she said something that changed my perspective and the course of my life. As I discussed school with her, I wasn't sure at the time about going. "After all," I said to her, "I'll be fifty by the time I graduate!" To which she replied, "So, you'll be fifty anyway." Oh. Hmmm. Great point. Never thought about it like that. In that simple statement, this over 40-year-old found some healing. You may not call it "miraculous" but God knew that was exactly what I needed to hear. Letting that thought sink in freed me from excuses, fears and doubts about getting older, or about having purpose in life." Stacy now has a seminary degree. You might be one of those women who should get one too!

88   In Carol Noren's book, *The Woman in the Pulpit* (Abingdon Press, 1992), Noren observes that when women present a familiar text, they often emphasize aspects of it that were previously unnoticed or deemed unimportant by male preachers. In other words, women see things that men don't, and vice versa.

agreeing wholeheartedly with each other, loving one another, and
working together with one mind and purpose.

Don't be selfish; don't try to impress others. Be humble, thinking
of others as better than yourselves. Don't look out only for your
own interests, but take an interest in others, too.

You must have the same attitude that Christ Jesus had.

Every generation has its unique challenges. One of ours, in the Twenty-
first Century church is to address the inequality and injustice of women within
the church and around the globe—and to get closer to shalom living. Over
the years, young seminary women have come seeking advice on how address
"the women's issue" in their faith communities. These women are educated
and have heard their whole life they could do and be whatever they wanted.
When these women enter the church and hear something different, they can
get their "hackles" up. I advise them to be like the children of Issachar. In 1
Chronicles 12:33 we read: "And the children of Issachar, who were men who
had understanding of the times, to know what Israel ought to do…"

About this passage, Dr. Dan Haydan writes: "The word understanding
is the Hebrew word *binah*, which means 'to have insight or to act with pru-
dence.' According to Strong's Concordance, it comes from a root verb that
means to separate something mentally, and distinguish its parts. The word
reflects the presence of intelligence and wisdom, even cunning and skill, in
the process. In other words, this is not just an understanding of the facts, but
a skillful analysis of what something truly means."[89]

Coming in with an attitude of "I am woman, hear me roar" is not wise
for many reasons. It shuts men down—especially men who have been
taught "at all costs don't lose to a girl." Also, many conservative Christians
have been socialized to view assertive women as feminists, a dirty word in
our strain of Christianity. But mostly, this attitude is unwise because Jesus
didn't adopt this.

---

89   www.awordfromtheword.org/understanding,

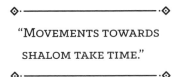

"MOVEMENTS TOWARDS
SHALOM TAKE TIME."

Women of Issachar must know the current wars against the truth, and discern what to do. In my opinion, God is on the move, bringing about global change for women. A movement is happening. But movements towards shalom take time. I'm mindful of the 400-plus years the Israelites waited in Egypt's womb before God birthed them into a nation. Though we consider Martin Luther's nailing his ninety-five theses on the Wittenburg door in 1517 the beginning of the Protestant Reformation, in truth, the movement started decades before the door. We see this in our own Civil Rights movement and the Women's movement. They occurred over a long period of time. Movements towards shalom take time. It's crucial we understand those times and know how we fit into them.

At this time in God's movement I see change. But we have a long way to go until God brings full shalom. I suspect I'll die before I see women functioning as full partners in the blessed alliance. My daughter might witness it, but I doubt I will. I'm not trying to be morbid or negative; it's just the reality of the times. I trust Jesus in his timing. I trust the Word of God, which says:

> For still the vision awaits its appointed time; it hastens to the end—it will not lie. If it seems slow, wait for it; it will surely come; it will not delay (Habakkuk 2:3 ESV).

> Wait for the Lord; be strong, and let your heart take courage; wait for the Lord! (Psalm 27:14).

There's peace in knowing you're not in charge but rather a tiny piece in God's huge story. Women of Issachar have the peace Jesus left us with (John 14:27).

With that said, let's get back to what we can do while we wait. After all, Galatians 6:9 says: "And let us not grow weary of doing good, for in due season we will reap, if we do not give up" (ESV).

—

I spent four days in a place I didn't belong: the UN Commission on the Status of Women. Distinguished dignitaries, politicians, and international organizations from around the world—and me! I felt I had little to contribute, but I gained understanding of our times and discernment on what we can do to reshape our view of women in conservative churches.

At a breakout session called "Religious Fundamentalism Gender Equality & Development," panelists spoke on the rise of fundamentalism within the major faiths (Christianity, Judaism, Buddhism, and Islam). Fundamentalism, they argued, rises out of deprivation and disorientation.[90] It's these conditions that foster fundamentalism, because at its core, fundamentalism provides very certain answers, very clear and rigid roles, and laws (many times they are enforced through dress codes). The panelists gave suggestions on how to break the chokehold of fundamentalism. One was to support those within the local community who are progressive in their thoughts and actions. Another was to offer theological conversations where people can become informed and make informed decisions about a particular theological issue.

The example given was divorce within Islamic fundamentalists. The suggestion was to read where divorce is addressed in the Koran and then dialogue over the way different Imams interpret those passages. The dialogue is

---

90   When fundamentalism is "full blown," it dehumanizes (excludes) those who don't follow the rules and roles. When you exclude certain people from humanity they become expendable (as evidenced with ISIS and Boko Haram). I'm thankful I live in American at a time in history where American Fundamentalism isn't "full blown." But the seminar did make me question those churches I know who have such rigid rules, dress codes, and role distinctions. I wondered if those churches were a reaction to a time of disorientation from the women's movement, science, the industrial revolution etc. I've read several of Dr. Michael Kimmel's books on men and masculinity. (Dr. Kimmel is considered one of the leading researchers on the subject). Kimmel states the women's movement left men disoriented because women took on characteristics that had traditionally been defined as male qualities. Men haven't known how to redefine themselves—yet. This may be an indicator as to why male-driven churches like Mars Hill (formerly under the leadership of Mark Driscoll) drew such crowds.

a way to provide the people with different opinions and allow them to come to their own conclusions.

I wanted to jump up and down and scream, "We've been doing that very thing with our women."

It started in 2006, when our women's ministry invited women theologians with differing opinions to discuss a hot topic like, "What do 'head' and 'submission' mean in the Bible?" Women witnessed other women thinking theologically and communicating truth with clarity. The idea wasn't to give our women all the answers so much as to help them develop critical thinking skills towards spiritual issues. It was from this model we developed the idea of the Marcella Project Salons. Our dialogues in women's ministry provoked water cooler conversations among church staff and lay people. It wasn't long before the men wanted in on the discussion.

Jill Briscoe once told me, "Jackie, do what you do well, and it will be hard for the church to ignore it." If we want to reshape our view of women, we start by knowing what we know—well. Become informed and carry out causal conversations and watch the water-cooler effect dribble down.

When we become humbly confident in our knowledge, skill, and God's vision, we start to live in new narrative.[91] Aligning ourselves with God's view of women ultimately reshapes our view of men too. Our brothers will no longer be seen as our enemies or superiors but rather as our allies and partners.[92] It's helpful to realize, when dealing with the men in leadership, that they know little about the unique challenges we face as women in ministry—or in

---

91   The *Harvard Business Review* ran an article titled, "Women Rising: The Unseen Barriers," in which they state something similar: "People become leaders by internalizing a leadership identity and developing a sense of purpose. (Herminia Ibarra, Robin Ely, and Deborah Kolb, *Harvard Business Review*, September 2013, p. 60).

92   At the U.N. Commission on the Status of Women in 2015, an Indian woman shared how her village campaigned young boys in order to raise awareness about the tradition of child brides. Once the boys were aware of the bondage it placed on young girls they began to argue with their parents about selling off their sisters as child brides. The boys became the girl's allies; change of heart, mind, thinking and tradition in the village, in the home.

the world. They have even less knowledge of the gender injustice inflicted upon women and girls around the globe. They are not cold-hearted, just uninformed.

As sisters, we must raise their awareness about women. To do that, ask: How can you put yourself in places and spaces where male leadership is present? How can you serve with male leadership? Have you asked to attend the leadership meetings? You might find they are open but just never thought of it. Have you made an argument for why women are vital to the leadership of a ministry? Make a case for the importance of a woman in leadership to represent the sixty-one percent of women in their church. Have you made a case for being paid? Would we expect a man to give forty hours a week to develop a men's ministry without pay? Scripture says a person's work is worth a fair wage: "The elders who direct the affairs of the church well are worthy of double honor, especially those whose work is preaching and teaching" (1 Timothy 5:17, 18).

During one of the breakouts at the U.N., an Albanian politician noted men treat women with more respect when they have money and power. If he's correct, then wouldn't our male leadership respect us more for seeing our work as worthy of financial reward? Again we approach these areas in our work place with a heart of humility and intention to serve the Body of Christ better. And please, let's be fully embodied females but never use our sexuality as a tool for influence, power, or control. It's obvious to all of us that we want to communicate we are sisters who aren't a threat to anyone's morality.

When the opportunity affords, share stories of women. Not like a saleswoman, but rather as a sister sharing Jesus' heart towards his Imago Dei—women. We've journeyed through my story, and you've read how the male staff responded to Shelley's story, so now: what stories can you share? Perhaps it's about a woman on staff or a laywoman who gives her time and talent, or maybe it's one of the women to whom you've been ministering, and her story needs to be told. It might be a story about a female CEO whose gifting suits a specific need in the church. Be sure to share stories from the color wheel—light pink stories as well as lime green and scarlet purple ones. We want men to be aware of the full scope of womanhood.

Here's one example of the rippling effect of sharing stories: Lauri was a volunteer for a recovery program at our church. She is a good leader with a great sense of humor. That's how our staff knew Lauri. What they didn't know was when she was fourteen she ran away from home and ended up at a bar where she was gang raped. That trauma sent her spiraling into a life of drugs and sexual exploitation. Jesus saved her from her attempts to end it all. Eventually, she got clean and gave her life to helping other women out of the sex industry. It wasn't long after our brothers heard Lauri's story that she found herself on the Sunday morning stage sharing it. After the service, two married couples approached Lauri. They were in shock. They had no idea what a life of a stripper[93] was like, in fact they attended strip clubs—together as couples—for fun. It didn't take long for what's considered a "woman's issue" to become a church-wide issue. Ripples continued. The men in our church raised funds for the removal of a tattoo branded on one sex slave's neck by her pimp. These men created a redemptive moment for her and in the process received redemption themselves. Men confessed they had frequented strip bars. They had had no idea about the life of a stripper either. There was repentance and freedom.

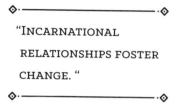

"INCARNATIONAL RELATIONSHIPS FOSTER CHANGE. "

It's crucial while bringing up these stories to not shame our brothers for the atrocities done to women by men. Men disassociate themselves from images of men being violent or sexually exploitive. Our job as sisters is to champion our brothers to their highest calling as Imago Dei-men. But that doesn't mean we shy away from the tough stories. Incarnational relationships foster change.

---

93 Thirteen is the average age teen trafficking begins, more than ninety percent of exploited women are victims of childhood sex abuse; ninety-six percent have been physically abused; eighty-seven percent have been abandoned; and eighty percent have run away from trouble and fatherless homes. (Stats from New Friends New Life, a ministry that helps women out of the sex industry, www.youtube.com/watch?v=ADpd_apiX78&feature=youtu.be)

How can you equip men to know the issues women face? How can you put other women's gifting and service in front of them? How can you consciously communicate you live in a different narrative than danger and romance? Tell men women's stories, and watch their views of women become reshaped.

—

John Quincy Adams said, "If your actions inspire others to dream more, learn more, do more, and become more, you are a leader."[94] Silly as this may sound, I've never really viewed myself as a leader. But regardless of how we see ourselves, other women are watching our work—work that inspires them to dream, learn, and become more.

I met Amy while I was speaking at a conservative retreat center in Upstate New York. One afternoon, during a break, we sat on a dock overlooking the lake that was nestled down among the towering Adirondack Mountains. As I listened to Amy's story, I realized God had set her apart for ministry. Not as a musician, as she might think, but as a teacher of the Word. As I shared my story of going from farm girl to preacher, Amy started to dream more for herself. Amy writes:

> In the midst of a time when God was calling me to pursue a deeper level of training in theology and speaking, I crossed paths with a renegade woman who broke all kinds of "rules," yet relentlessly loved Jesus unlike anyone I had ever seen before. Her daring and risky way of pursuing what God had called her to unveiled possibilities I had honestly never considered before. Not only through her example, but also through her direct encouragement to me specifically, I am halfway through an M.Div. program. I would have never thought I was worthy, capable, or "allowed" to go to seminary without her input in my life, yet as I study Hebrew and homiletics my heart soars. I'm flourishing in what I was created to do!

94 www.goodreads.com/author/quotes/117066.John_Quincy_Adams

Some days at my ultra-conservative, male-dominated seminary are challenging, but I persevere and see God opening doors in random and fantastically beautiful ways.

Amy wasn't the only woman encouraged to dream because of IBC's new view of women. A year or so after preaching, a professor from Dallas Theological Seminary shared how there had been a shift among women on campus. Ministry possibilities that female students once considered "off limits" were being entertained. Dreaming was happening. Equipping was occurring. But it didn't just impact other seminary women. Listen to what one stay-at-home mom wrote.

Dear Jackie,

I've been meaning to tell you how much I have enjoyed hearing you preach.

I did not grow up in the evangelical church and came from a family that taught me to be a strong, vocal, assertive woman who believed there were no limits in life. I became a believer in college, but quickly realized I wasn't the "right" kind of Christian woman. Once I started attending evangelical churches, I came to understand that women were somewhat limited in the ways they were to serve the Body. I honestly didn't have a huge chip on my shoulder about this, because most of the time I felt like women were treated with dignity and respect.

As long as our limitations were demonstrations of humility and not a lack of intellect or ability, it didn't really matter to me that women weren't preaching on Sunday mornings. So imagine my surprise when I first heard you preach. Suddenly, it mattered to me! It wasn't just that your teaching was insightful and moving (though it was). It was that I was able to connect to the message in a way I never had before. I've heard you teach in Bible study many times and have always loved your teaching, but to hear you in "big church" was incredibly moving and important.

I just wanted to encourage you because I'm certain that you've gotten some flack. If hearing a woman preach caused such a reaction in me—someone who admittedly has never given much pause to this limitation—I can only imagine how this will effect women who have been turned off by the church because they felt like their voices were literally never heard. What you're doing matters, Jackie, and I'm so thankful that you've been brave enough to speak.

Women in our faith communities need women role models—light pink ones and lime green too. Think about this woman's letter. She didn't even realize the impact of hearing a female voice teach the Scriptures from a female experience. This woman didn't realize, but what about the other women in the pews who do realize? Ninety-five percent of senior pastors and approximately seventy percent of worship leaders are male. Rarely do women see other women pray publically or hold a Bible on the stage or collect the offering or lead a mixed-gender meeting or even open a mixed-gender meeting in prayer.

Instead, we see mostly light pink service and sanction it as if it's how God made women to serve. Kenneth Woodward, religion reporter said, "Women predominate in churches, in part because they mostly carry out the important role of nurturing and catechizing children."[95]

David Murrow, an elder and author on the feminized church, said men are more wired "for action and argument rather than contemplation and polite discussion."[96]

Light pink is preferred. But what do we do with women like me or Amy or Shelley or Ruth, Huldah, Priscilla, Deborah, Miriam, Tamar, or *you*? [97]

---

95   archive.decaturdaily.com/decaturdaily/religion/060701/church.shtml

96   archive.decaturdaily.com/decaturdaily/religion/060701/church.shtml

97   Forty percent of women say they have more opportunity to lead outside their church than within their church. www.slideshare.net/ERWWNewConsumer/gender-shift-the-millennial-generation-6892308

As I wrote earlier, a recent Barna study showed that for the first time in twenty years, women are leaving the church.[98] I would argue it's partially because we have few role models beyond light pink. We need women, light pink, lime green, and whichever shade you are to model what it looks like to live, love, and serve Jesus with every fiber of our being—within our faith communities.

———

My mind drifts back to that day in chapel when that tall, elegant women stood up and preached God's Word (in her English accent) in front of male and female students and professors. As she preached Scripture, something happened inside. I had a burning, exciting sensation in my belly and tears rolled down my face. I didn't fully understand what I experienced but watching her courage and listening to her preaching skill shaped me. Women are sitting in your chapel, so to speak, and whether you realize it or not, they are being shaped by your service to Jesus. Let your color shine so they can dream, learn, and become more fully their own color.

One final word to the wise: remember we don't follow an *idea*. We follow a Person. Too often, when something is costly, we can slip from following the Person to the idea. Richard Rohr said it like this: "We all become a well-disguised mirror image of anything we fight too long or too directly. That which we oppose determines the energy and frames the questions after a while. You lose all your inner freedom."[99]

A friend once said she strongly defended homeschooling as the "best" way to raise kids because she homeschooled her children. The experience had been so costly, she imagined it *had* to be the best way. Otherwise, why did she sacrifice so much?

Ugh. I resemble that.

By late 2009, I knew I needed to slow down, step back. Twice I went to the emergency room with blood pressure at the stroke level. The stress I had

---

98   www.patheos.com/blogs/jesuscreed/2014/12/09/why-are-women-leaving-the-church/

99   Richard Rohr, *Falling Upward*, (San Francisco: Jossey-Bass, 2011) p. 118.

carried for so long started to take its toll. Four different doctors said to lower my stress or I would die. But I didn't know how. People were counting on me. Women were watching and dreaming. I thought, *If I step back, will our church go backward and stop championing the cause for women?*

You see the red flags, don't you? Somewhere—and I have no idea where—I slipped from following Jesus to following an idea. That's my nice way of saying I had fallen into idolatry. To worship means "devote yourself to" to "give worth to." Glorify, remember, means "to give weight to, credit, praise to." Everyone who serves in ministry walks a thin line. We start with sincere intentions: we worship Jesus. But at some point, the work becomes more important than the Person of Jesus Christ. Oh, I know: we would never say that, and I suspect many of us aren't even aware that we've crossed the line. Until, that is, God pulls the rug out from under us.

In November of 2010 my husband was unexpectedly fired.[100] It was sudden and sloppy (a nice way of saying "not done well"!), and we were floored. Overnight our whole life turned on its head. Our jobs, finances, home, children, friendships—all flipped in a moment's time. Sometimes God pulls the rug out[101] from us to reveal just who or what we are worshipping.

In Psalm 29,[102] verse by verse, God slaps around these false gods that the Israelites were tempted to worship. God's basically saying, "I know you. You

---

100   I continued to serve at IBC for another year. Yes, it was hard, but I believe God is capable of resurrection. Unfortunately, after a year, I knew it was not time for healing to occur on the staff level. God would bring reconciliation at another time.

101   I'm not saying the reason for all trials is to reveal idolatry, but sometimes they are.

102   Ascribe to the LORD, O heavenly beings·ascribe to the LORD glory and strength. Ascribe to the LORD the glory due his name; worship the LORD in the splendor of holiness. The voice of the LORD is over the waters; the God of glory thunders, the LORD, over many waters. The voice of the LORD is powerful; the voice of the LORD is full of majesty. The voice of the LORD breaks the cedars; the LORD breaks the cedars of Lebanon. He makes Lebanon to skip like a calf, and Sirion like a young wild ox. The voice of the LORD flashes forth flames of fire. The voice of the LORD shakes the wilderness; the LORD shakes the wilderness of Kadesh. The voice of the LORD makes the deer give birth·and strips the forests bare, and in his temple all cry, "Glory!" The LORD sits enthroned over the flood; the LORD sits enthroned as king forever. May the LORD give strength to his people! May the LORD bless his people with peace! —*Psalm 29 ESV*

are tempted to worship these false gods. But 'the voice of the LORD breaks the cedars of Lebanon.' Do you see me? I'm throwing them around like they are nothing. They are not worthy of your worship. Only I AM is worthy of your worship" (my paraphrase—obviously!).

Psalm 29 is God pulling the rug out from underneath the Israelites. And sometimes he pulls it out from underneath us too. Because somewhere along the way, many times without our even noticing, we've come to devote ourselves to another.

Job

Relationships

Children

Legacy

Reputation

Program

Retirement fund

Our reshaping the view of women

None of these are bad things. It's just somewhere along the way we give them more weight than we should. God said, "Thou shall have no other gods before me" so he pulls the rug from underneath our feet. Idols crash. Eyes open. Revelation. *Now* realignment can occur.

It took a few years. While God worked on my heart, a friend and I worked to launch The Marcella Project, a ministry committed to ennobling women, in 2012. I'm grateful for those who carried me through the healing process, who kept my passions alive while Jesus brought me home to single-minded devotion—again. Grieving and healing takes time,[103] but I came out the

---

103 A helicopter landed on a busy street corner right near my house. A woman had been in an accident and they airlifted her to a hospital. It took all of forty-five minutes to land the helicopter, load the woman, clean up the accident so traffic could fully resume. I remember observing that incident and thinking, "That's how we do grieving in America and in the church, slam, bam, done." Ugh.

other side with my eyes locked back on Jesus. I'm so grateful for pulled rugs. I am still just as passionate about reshaping our view of women. I still give my time, talent, and treasure to ennobling women. But I know I'm not the only one God has on the job. Remember when the Prophet Elijah ran from Jezebel in fear of his life. He complained to God that he was the only one left who hadn't bowed to Baal and God tells him, "Hey, I've got it covered. There are 7,000 others who haven't bowed either" (my paraphrase of 1 Kings 19: 1–18). And I'm not the one who brings in the Kingdom of God. God does. It's his. And he said, "It is finished" (John 19:30).

My passion is still to ennoble women. It's just not my end all be all— Jesus is.

And he promises to be all for us. Ezekiel 37:27 assures us that God will be our God, and we will be his people. We will be his women. No matter how winding or treacherous the road that brought us to God. No matter which shade of pink or green or dazzling purple. We are his. He is ours.

It seems appropriate to end this story here.

Jackie,
Ennobler of women

A Note from Jackie

I n 2012, I founded **The Marcella Project** with the help of many friends to ennoble women through Scripture-focused teaching, training, and dialogue. The ministry started small with Bible studies in wineries. We wanted to create a safe space for women to connect with each other and engage with Jesus. The local winery—casual, organic, ordinary—cultivated the authenticity women were longing to encounter at a Bible study.

We also wanted to foster healthy dialogue on tough topics, encouraging both critical thinking and candid conversation. Salons were born: intimate gatherings for informed conversations on spiritual issues impacting women's lives. Equipping women with the skills and confidence needed to teach Scripture effectively was the final piece. So we set out to train women in my *She Can Teach* course, empowering them to teach God's Word in a way that ennobles women – dignifying them and lifting them up to nobility, just as Jesus intended.

The Marcella Project has grown into more than a ministry. We are a movement to ennoble women. Together we are transforming the way women view themselves and the way the faith community views women, so that the Church can change what's happening to women and girls around the world. I'd love to invite you to join us as an ennobler of women.

Visit **marcellaproject.com** to learn more about The Marcella Project, shop our online store for Bible study guides, books, and other resources that ennoble women, or register for one of our upcoming Bible studies, Salons, or *She Can Teach* trainings. Send us a message at admin@themarcellaproject.com to hire a TMP speaker for a conference, speaking event, training, or salon.

If you'd like to be a part of our team, consider joining **The Marcella 100** —a collective voice fighting for a proper view and standing for all women worldwide. We're building a team of learners, ambassadors, and funders of our mission to ennoble women. Visit marcellaproject.com/member to join or learn more.

Whatever it looks like for you—thank you for ennobling women in your everyday life. It glorifies Jesus in every way.

Empowering Women to Teach Scripture Effectively